MRCGP:

Approaching the New Modular Examination

Edited and Compiled
by

JOHN SANDARS
FRCGP MRCP (UK)

Diploma in Palliative Medicine,
Diploma in Counselling,
Certificate in Education,
General Practitioner and Trainer, Cheadle Hulme,
Stockport and Handforth, Cheshire.
Examiner MRCGP examination

PasTest Revision Books and Intensive Courses
PasTest has been established in the field of postgraduate medical education since 1972, providing revision books and intensive study courses for doctors preparing for their professional examinations. Books and courses are available for the following specialties:
MRCP Part 1 and Part 2 (General Medicine and Paediatrics),
MRCOG, DRCOG, MRCGP, DCH, FRCA, FRCS, PLAB.
For further details contact:
PasTest, Freepost, Knutsford, Cheshire WA16 7BR
Tel: 01565 755226 Fax: 01565 650264

Text prepared and printed by MFP Design & Print, Longford Trading Estate, Thomas Street, Stretford, Manchester M32 0JT, UK.

CONTENTS

PREFACE

This book is not a textbook of General Practice, nor is it a last minute examination crammer. It offers a systematic approach to the MRCGP examination, providing the candidate with an invaluable insight into what the examiners are looking for and how to answer questions in order to gain the maximum marks. Several practice papers with answers are provided to help in this process.

The MRCGP examination has recently undergone a major review and the new modular examination seems likely to be present for the next few years. The Royal College is constantly trying to improve the validity and reliability of the examination and minor changes may be introduced. Every effort has been made to ensure that this new book contains the most up to date information that is currently available.

The debate between the relationship of Summative Assessment and the MRCGP examination continues and in the near future it is expected that it will be more clearly defined.

This new edition would not have been possible without the help of several of my fellow examiners:

Sean Coughlin	Current Awareness type questions
Nick Foster	Critical Appraisal type questions
Moya Kelly	Problem-solving type questions
Paul Middleton	Critical Appraisal type questions
Val Wass	Oral Examinations

I thank Richard Bircher for sharing his experiences as a registrar preparing for the examination — and his success.

I would like to express my thanks to John Foulkes and the Examinations Department of the RCGP for their support and kind permission to reproduce several items.

Finally I would like to thank the publishing department at PasTest since without their help the book would never have reached publication!

I hope that you find this book helpful and I wish you every success — not just in the MRCGP examination but in your future in general practice.

John Sandars

INTRODUCTION TO THE MRCGP EXAMINATION

The MRCGP examination has constantly evolved since it was first developed in 1965. The examination is set by the Royal College of General Practitioners as an 'assessment of the knowledge, skills and attitudes appropriate to the General Practitioner on completion of vocational training, assessing the competence of candidates to carry out unsupervised responsibility for the care of patients in general practice'. Although, at approximately 70%, the overall pass rate is higher than that of other postgraduate medical examinations, the MRCGP exam cannot be described as easy and should not be taken lightly.

The structure of the examination

The MRCGP exam is now modular, using a credit accumulation system. The main features of this new style examination are as follows:

1. Candidates must pass all 4 modules in order to pass the examination overall.
2. The modules may be taken at the same session, or at different sessions, and in any order. For example, candidates do not have to pass the written papers before taking the oral.
3. Candidates may have up to 2 further attempts at each module (on payment of a supplementary fee).
4. All modules must be passed within 3 years of acceptance of the application, otherwise the entire examination has to be retaken.

The four modules of the examination are:

- Paper 1 (examiner marked)
- Paper 2 (machine marked)
- An assessment of consulting skills
- Oral examination

Each module is available twice a year, in the summer and in the winter.

Paper 1 and Paper 2

There are two written papers and each is available twice a year. They are timetabled on the same day for the convenience of those candidates who want to take both papers at the same session, but they can be taken or retaken singly. Paper 1 is held in the morning and Paper 2 in the afternoon.

Consulting skills

Consulting skills will be assessed by one of two methods:

1. A video recording of the candidate consulting with patients who have given their consent to be recorded.
2. The candidate takes part in a 'simulated surgery' in which the candidate consults with a sequence of actors who play the part of patients.

Video recording is the normal method of assessing consulting skills for the MRCGP and the simulated surgery is available only to those candidates who, in the opinion of the examiners, have insuperable difficulties in making video recordings; for example if the candidate is practising in an area where most consultations are conducted in a language other than English. Special application has to be made to the Examinations Department when a simulated surgery is requested.

At the time of applying for the Consulting Skills module the candidate must submit a valid and completed certificate of competence in child health surveillance.

The oral examination

Candidates are assigned to a centre, either London or Edinburgh, for an oral examination.

Application for the MRCGP examination

All candidates must provide evidence of proficiency in basic cardiopulmonary resuscitation and child health surveillance at the time of application for the examination. There are other eligibility criteria, such as the length of time in practice and appropriate experience. Full details are available from the **Examinations Department, Royal College of General Practitioners, 14 Princes Gate, Hyde Park, London, SW7 1PU.**

Content of the examination

Every general practitioner is required to have a breadth of knowledge and skills rather than large amounts of in-depth knowledge about small topics — this is the realm of the specialist. The MRCGP examination reflects this requirement and the content has no strictly defined curriculum. Instead it sets out to test all of those areas that comprise good general practice in the British National Health Service today. Candidates who practise within a different system of health care should be aware of this British focus and will need to be prepared appropriately.

The examination overall is designed to test the **domains of competence** required of a contemporary general practitioner and also the various roles that a doctor may be required to adopt in the course of ordinary general practice.

The Domains of Competence

- Factual knowledge
- Evolving knowledge — current emerging areas/'hot topics'
- The evidence base of practice — knowledge of current literature
- Critical appraisal skills — interpretation of literature and principles of statistics
- Application of knowledge — problem solving and clinical decision making
- Personal care — matching principles to individual patients
- Written communication
- Verbal communication — the consultation process
- The practice context — practice management, business skills and team issues
- The regulatory framework of practice — medico-political, legal and societal issues
- Ethnic and transcultural issues
- Values and attitudes — ethics and integrity
- Self awareness — insight and 'the doctor as a person'
- Commitment to maintaining standards — personal and professional growth and continuing medical education

---

The Various Roles the Doctor may adopt

- Clinician and family physician
- The patient's advocate
- Resource allocator
- Team leader and team member
- Partner and colleague
- Employer and manager
- Teacher
- Researcher
- Member of the profession
- Reflective practitioner
- Individual person

The wide range of knowledge — the breadth of general practice — can be appreciated by considering the Five Areas of General Practice, which are found on page xiv. More details of this can be found in the publication *The Future General Practitioner — Learning and Teaching* which can be purchased directly from the Royal College of General Practitioners.

Each module of the examination is specifically designed to assess the candidate's performance in both the domains of competence and the role of the general practitioner.

Paper 1

Paper 1 is a three hour written paper which is marked by a group of examiners. Typically Paper 1 consists of twelve or more questions to be answered in 3 hours and each question makes an equal contribution to the result. There is an extra 30 minutes allowed so that candidates can read through any presented material. Candidates will be given a combined question and answer book with one page for each question and answers are to be written on the same sheet. Candidates will be expected to give legible and concise answers but short note form is acceptable. Occasionally candidates will be required to give structured short answers in which the response is entered into a table or similar fixed format.

The completed booklet is split up and each page is sent to a different examiner. Candidates are therefore advised to answer each question independently, even if this involves repetition of part of an earlier answer.

There are four main types of question.

1. Questions designed to test knowledge and interpretation of general practice literature. The questions will normally take the form of a direct instruction to discuss and/or evaluate the current views on a topic and the general evidence on which they are based.

The approach to this type of question is described in the section 'Approach to Current Awareness Type Questions' on page 73.

2. Questions that test the candidate's ability to evaluate and interpret written material. This material may be in the form of published papers or extracts from papers, such as summaries or methods and results sections on their own. It may also include meta-analyses, structured summaries, leading articles from journals or systemic reviews.

The approach to this type of question is outlined in the section 'Approach to Critical Appraisal Type Questions' on page 1.

3. Questions that examine the candidate's ability to integrate and apply theoretical knowledge and professional values within the setting of primary health care in the United Kingdom. These questions test the candidate's practical approach to general practice problems and marks are gained for the management of the problem rather than for the factual knowledge.

The approach to this type of question is described in the section 'Approach to Modified Essay Question (Problem Solving) Type Questions' on page 83.

4. New question formats. Other question formats may appear from time to time. This is part of the naturally evolving process of ensuring that the examination is both valid (i.e. measuring what it hopes to measure) and reliable (i.e. that it measures consistently).

Paper 2

This paper is designed to test the candidate's knowledge, both established and recent, about general practice. A multiple choice question format provides an ideal method of assessing a candidate's knowledge base; the application of this knowledge can be assessed by problem solving and extended matching type questions. The paper is machine marked and candidates will be required to answer a maximum of 400 true/false items and 100 items of the extended matching or problem solving variety. Answers are recorded on machine marked sheets. This paper is of 3 hours duration. Questions which are accompanied by reading material or a table to appraise should be done early in the exam as they take longer to do than the standard true/false questions and may cause the candidate to rush them if they are left until the end of the examination.

The approach to this type of question is described in the section 'Approach to Multiple Choice and Computer Marked Questions' on page 111.

Oral examination

This consists of two consecutive oral examinations, each lasting 20 minutes and each conducted by two different pairs of examiners. This part of the examination assesses the candidate's decision-making ability, and the professional values underpinning it.

The approach to this section is outlined in 'Approach to the Oral Examination Component' on page 188.

Assessment of consulting skills

Candidates are expected to submit evidence of competence in consulting skills in the form of a video recording of a sample of their recent consultations, accompanied by a completed workbook. The workbook contains a videotape log, consultation assessment forms and detailed evaluation forms. Candidates are expected to submit 15 consultations, with five presented as detailed evaluations. In exceptional circumstances candidates may be able to take part in a simulated surgery.

Further details of both of these methods can be found in the section 'Approach to the Assessment of Consulting Skills Component — Video and Simulated Surgery' on pages 199 and 211.

The results

The result in each of the four modules will be reported as fail, pass or pass with merit. Approximately 25% of candidates scoring the highest marks in each module will be given a pass with merit for that module. To achieve a pass in the MRCGP examination overall, candidates must achieve at least a pass in all four modules within three years of the acceptance of the application. If this is not achieved the candidate will be deemed to have failed the examination as a whole. Candidates can be awarded an overall pass with merit and it is possible to be awarded an overall pass with distinction. The various rules regarding the attempts allowed at each module and how the overall result is calculated can be obtained directly from the Examinations Department of the Royal College of General Practitioners.

THE FIVE AREAS OF GENERAL PRACTICE

The MRCGP exam syllabus covers a great breadth of knowledge and the exam itself aims to measure knowledge, skills and attitudes within the Five Areas of General Practice.

1. Clinical practice — health and disease

The candidate will be required to demonstrate knowledge of the diagnosis, management and, where appropriate, the prevention of diseases of importance in general practice. This area includes:

- The range of normal
- The patterns of illness
- The natural history of diseases
- Prevention
- Early diagnosis
- Diagnostic methods and techniques
- Management and treatment.

2. Clinical practice — human development

The candidate will be expected to possess knowledge of human development and be able to demonstrate the value of this knowledge in the diagnosis and management of patients in general practice. This area includes:

- Genetics
- Fetal development
- Physical development in childhood, maturity and ageing
- Intellectual development in childhood, maturity and ageing
- Emotional development in childhood, maturity and ageing
- The range of normal.

3. Clinical practice — human behaviour

The candidate must demonstrate an understanding of human behaviour, particularly as it affects the presentation and management of disease. This area includes:

- Behaviour presenting to the general practitioner
- Behaviour in interpersonal relationships
- Behaviour of the family
- Behaviour in the doctor – patient relationship.

4. Medicine and society

The candidate must be familiar with the common sociological and epidemiological concepts and their relevance to medical care and must be able to demonstrate knowledge of the organisation of medical and related services in the United Kingdom and abroad. This area includes:

- Sociological aspects of health and illness
- The uses of epidemiology
- The organisation of medical care in the UK and comparisons with other countries
- The relationship of medical services to other institutions of society.

5. The practice

The candidate must demonstrate a knowledge of practice organisation and administration and must be able to discuss recent developments in the evolution of general practice critically. This area includes:

- Practice management
- The team
- Financial matters
- Premises and equipment
- Medical records
- Medico-legal matters
- Research.

REVISION PLANNING

A planned approach to revision is the key to getting through the MRCGP exam.

The most important point to remember is that this is an exam about **current general practice** and your reading needs to reflect this. Subjects such as general medicine, obstetrics and paediatrics are included but they only make up a small proportion. In order to put this in perspective, it is helpful to look carefully at the Five Areas of General Practice on the preceding pages. You can see from this that:

Area 1: Health and disease encompasses most of the areas covered in finals and found in textbooks.

Area 2: Human development covers paediatrics but also includes knowledge of the elderly.

Area 3: Human behaviour is an important area in general practice. It covers such areas as: why patients present, consultation models, the doctor – patient relationship and interpersonal relationships as they affect patients, their families and doctors.

Area 4: Medicine and society covers the epidemiology and sociology of health care, for example knowledge of the cause of disease (e.g. cholesterol and CHD risk). This is vital to our methods of treating such disease. This area includes the organisation of health care — a subject that has been affecting all of us recently.

Area 5: The practice includes knowledge of practice management (e.g. finances, records, premises). It also includes general management skills such as delegation, time management and team development.

Covering all these areas in your revision will give you the broad knowledge base required for the exam and for life as a GP (which is, of course, what the exam is designed to do!).

At first glance, the amount of work required can seem immense but by working through the different areas logically you will see that you already have a lot of the knowledge required. Your revision plan needs to be designed to fill the gaps. You will not fail for not understanding the cost-rent scheme (although you should know how to find out about it). You may however be on shaky ground if you know nothing about the management of a practice.

It is also important to remember that the exam reflects *current* practice and *current* research, not out-of-date books.

Bearing all this in mind, how can you start to cover the material?

Textbooks

You may need to read selected textbooks to cover areas in which your knowledge is deficient (e.g. on the doctor – patient relationship or practice management). If you feel that you are lacking in basic medical knowledge, it may be worth reading a textbook but bear in mind all the other areas of knowledge as well. It is worth reading something on the common diseases in general practice. A recommended reading list is given in Appendix 5.

Journals

These cover the current research in general practice. *The British Journal of General Practice* and the *British Medical Journal* are essential reading, preferably for the 12 –18 months up to the exam (remember the written exam is set in the Spring). This task may seem daunting – but is actually very interesting! You do not need to read everything. It is worth keeping notes on what you have read as it is useful to be able to review them as the exam date approaches. Look especially for review articles and recurrent 'topical' themes.

Other journals such as *Update* and *Monitor* are worth perusing as they often contain subjects not covered elsewhere, but be selective. Beware of the common fault of reading articles on subjects you already understand well.

Reading one of the weekly medical newspapers, such as *Doctor*, *Pulse* or *General Practitioner* can give a good overview of the current developments in general practice.

Occasional papers and reports from general practice

These are the current literature of general practice and hence include some vital reading. There is a list of important articles on pages 81-82. It is worth being aware of recent publications as these are often clues to current areas of importance in general practice.

As the amount of work can seem daunting, the best approach is to divide up the list between a group of people and ask each person to produce a short summary (i.e. 1 – 3 typed A4 sheets) on the paper or report which can then be shared.

Current affairs

Newspapers, television and radio will keep you up to date and aware of current issues. The media often present subjects from a different perspective which can be useful.

Hot topics

Paradoxically, most of these have been around for some time and again it is a matter of broad reading and being aware of current initiatives to make sure of covering them. A checklist is included in Appendix 6 to make sure you have not missed any major areas.

Planning

Go through the 'five areas' and the list of revision topics to identify a list of areas on which you want to concentrate. Start with those areas you know nothing about and, if there is time, come back to topics you know better. That way you will ensure a broad knowledge base.

Ideally, get together with other people taking the exam and share out topics and occasional papers to produce short summaries of each. When you read a topic, try to think about the sort of questions you could be asked, (e.g. managing a diabetic who will not accept his disease). Always think about the ethical issues. Remember, the difficult problems that arise in surgery are often the same ones that appear in the exam.

Practicing

Practicing the different components of the exam will improve your technique and help identify weak areas of knowledge.

Remember

- Doing, discussing and communicating are as important as sitting in a room reading
- Have an overall plan. Keep records of what you read as this helps revision and allows you to see progress from your efforts
- Steady reading throughout the year is better than pre-exam panic.

Good luck!

APPROACH TO CRITICAL APPRAISAL TYPE QUESTIONS

Increasingly all general practitioners are being faced with an array of material which has to be evaluated and interpreted. This component is found in both Paper 1 and Paper 2 and questions are designed to test the candidate's ability to do the following:

- Analyse and interpret an audit, consider change and apply these principles to real-life situations.
- Critically appraise presented material. This includes an ability to state the main types of design and methodology, to recognise the strengths and weaknesses of each, to identify the sources of bias and the effects made to eliminate bias and to identify the validity and reliability of studies.
- Interpret the results of presented material. This includes knowledge of power calculations, p values, confidence intervals, NNT (number needed to treat), odds ratios, sensitivity, specificity and predictive values.
- Apply the strength of evidence to a clinical scenario.
- Critically appraise systematic reviews, meta-analyses, cost-effective evaluations and guidelines.
- Apply an evidence based medicine approach to a clinical scenario including formulation of a question, search strategy, appraisal of evidence and application of evidence to the clinical problem.

How to approach critical appraisal questions

Critically appraising a clinical paper can seem a daunting prospect. However, a planned approach will make it easier.

The scope of this section is vast and only the basic principles are outlined here. Further details can be obtained by reference to the two excellent texts referred to in the recommended reading list: *Basic Epidemiology* by Beaglehole R, Bonita R and Kjellstrom T, World Health Organisation and *The Pocket Guide to Critical Appraisal* by Crombie I, BMJ Publishing Group.

Critical appraisal skills are used to assess the quality of research and evidence that should underpin our clinical decision making. Critical appraisal skills concentrate on two areas:

- Basic study design
- Basic statistical interpretation.

1. Basic study design

Typical study designs include the following:

Cross-sectional study — a survey of the frequency of the disease or the risk factor in a defined population at a given time. This can assess prevalence and may generate hypotheses about associations between risk factors and diseases, but it cannot evaluate hypotheses since it does not take into account how exposure to a risk factor relates to the development of the disease.

Cohort study — a type of observational study of a group of subjects with a specific disease or characteristic who are followed up over a period of time to detect complications or new events. This group may be compared with a control group. Often this type of study requires follow up over several years, and it may be prone to loss of subjects and recall bias.

Case control study — a type of observational study in which the characteristics of subjects with a disease are compared with a selected group of control subjects without the disease. The validity of this type of study depends on the appropriate selection of control subjects.

Controlled trial — an experimental study in which an intervention is applied to one group of subjects and the outcome compared with that in a control group who received another intervention, which may be active treatment or a placebo. Ideally patients should be assigned to treatment groups in a randomised manner. The randomised control trial is considered to be the 'gold standard'.

2. Basic statistical interpretation

Statistical tests can appear to be very complicated but the underlying principle to note is that these tests are used to quantify the likelihood that the observed result is a real effect rather than having arisen by chance.

There are several well recognised statistical tests that can be applied to data but detailed consideration of these is beyond the scope of this book. However, all of these tests are designed to assess the probability that observed differences could have risen purely by chance rather than through the intervention. Such tests of significance are discussed in the list of key terms on page 7.

Critical appraisal scheme for clinical trial papers

<u>Objectives and hypotheses</u>

- Can you identify clearly the objective(s) of the study?
- Do the investigators state or imply the population to which they intend to refer their findings?
- Given the above, are these important and relevant objectives?

<u>Design of the investigation</u>

- Is the design of the study suitable for the proposed objectives?
- How was the sample selected? Are there possible sources of selection bias, which would make the sample atypical, and if so is a provision made to deal with this bias?
- What was the response rate and was any attempt made to assess the characteristics of non-responders?
- Was some form of control necessary, and if so is it satisfactory?
- Are inclusion and exclusion criteria for the sample clearly defined and applied?
- Is the study large enough to achieve its objectives? For numerical estimates and comparisons appropriate power calculations should be described.
- If it is a clinical trial are there clear rules for withdrawal from or stopping the trial? Is there provision for detecting likely adverse events?
- If a randomisation design is desirable has it been used and adequately described?
- If it is a multi-centre trial does the organisation/co-ordination seem adequate?

<u>Measurement and observations</u>

- Are there clear definitions of the terms used, including diagnostic criteria, measurements and criteria of outcome?
- Are the measurements valid, i.e. accurate?
- Are the measurements repeatable, i.e. consistent over time and between different subjects, places of measurement, etc?
- Have attempts been made to minimise bias in the measurements? If bias is clearly unavoidable has it been evaluated?

Presentation of results

- Are the results presented clearly, objectively and in sufficient detail to enable readers to make their own judgement?
- Are the results internally consistent, i.e. do the numbers add up properly, and can the different tables be reconciled?

Analysis

- Are the data suitable for statistical analysis?
- Are the statistical methods stated and appropriate to the data?
- Are the statistical tests correctly performed and interpreted?
- Is there sufficient analysis to determine whether significant differences are in fact due to lack of comparability of the groups in age or sex, or in other relevant variables?

Discussion

- Are the results discussed in relation to existing knowledge on the subject and the study objectives?
- Is the discussion biased?

Conclusions

- Are the conclusions justified, given the methodology and results?

Style and presentation

- Is there a clear and unambiguous style and appropriate length?
- Is the journal that the paper has been published in appropriate to the likely readership? Is it a high circulation or specialist journal?
- Are the references appropriate and up to date and relevant to the study and the conclusions?

Critical appraisal scheme for review papers

Review papers such as systematic reviews or meta-analyses are becoming increasingly common since they summarise scientific evidence on a particular topic. Such reviews save the reader from searching and appraising a whole series of articles, but this very process can lead to bias. Critical appraisal of such review papers is increasingly important since for the busy reader these reviews provide the usual scientific evidence on which clinical decisions are made.

- Did the review address a clearly focused issue, related to the population studied, the intervention given or the outcomes considered?
- Were important and relevant studies included? Has there been a wide search for published and unpublished studies, in both non-English language and English language journals? Were appropriate databases searched and what were the search strategies?
- Have the authors of the review assessed the quality of the included studies? The quality of the review depends on the qualities of these original studies — if there are poor original studies then the review will draw inappropriate conclusions!
- Were the results similar from study to study?
- What is the overall result of the review?
- How precise are the results? Has there been statistical confirmation of precision?
- Can the results be applied to the local population? Are the patients covered by the review similar enough to the local population to which you wish to apply the results?
- Were all clinically important outcomes considered?
- Are the benefits worth the harms and costs?

Critical appraisal scheme for pharmaco-economic studies

- Have the study questions and hypothesis and design been clearly stated?
- Has the study involved a comparison of at least two alternatives? The 'do nothing', 'least-costly' and 'most-used' options should be considered.
- Have all relevant costs and benefits of the alternatives been identified and appropriately valued?
- Is the study of sufficient size to assess significant differences between alternatives?
- Have marginal costs and benefits of alternatives been valued?
- Have future costs and benefits been appropriately discounted?
- Has detailed sensitivity analysis been conducted?

Critical appraisal scheme for guidelines

- Have the authors responsible for the development of the guideline been clearly identified?
- Has external funding or support been received and if so has any potential bias been taken into account?
- Are the reasons for developing the guideline clearly stated?
- Is there a description of the individuals who are involved in developing the guideline and if so did the group contain representatives of all key disciplines?
- Is there a description of the sources of information used to select the evidence on which the recommendations are based and if so are they adequate?
- Is there a description of the methods used to interpret and assess the strength of the evidence?
- How was group consensus reached?
- Is there an adequate description of the health benefits that are likely to be gained from the recommended management and is there an adequate description of the cost:benefit ratio?
- Have the guidelines been piloted and independently reviewed by experts prior to release?
- Is there a mention of a date for reviewing or updating the guidelines?
- Is there a mention of other sets of guidelines that deal with the same topic, and if so, is there a discussion of differences between the guidelines and reasons for them?

- Is there a satisfactory description of the patients to which the guidelines are meant to apply?
- Is there a satisfactory description of the circumstances in which exceptions may be made to using the guidelines?
- Is there an explicit statement of how patient preferences should be taken into account in applying the guidelines?
- Are the guidelines clear in describing which condition is to be detected, treated or prevented?
- Are the recommendations clearly presented?
- Do the guidelines contain a dissemination strategy and is this realistic?
- Is there a statement of how the guidelines can be adapted to local use?
- Is it possible to identify standards clearly and can the guidelines be subject to audit?

Key terms used in critical appraisal and basic statistics

Bias — this refers to any methodological flaw likely to produce deviation from true observation or measurement.

- **Sample or selection bias** — in some way the sample is not representative of the population from which it comes
- **Recall bias** — e.g. inability to recall information related to exposure to risk factors, as in case-control studies
- **Non response bias** — when information only relates to the responders, who may not be representative of the population from which the sample is drawn. Non response bias becomes less important at response rates over about 70%.

Blindness — used to describe the lack of awareness of investigators and participants of their inclusion and whether they are part of treatment or control treatment groups in order to eliminate potential bias. In single blind trials the investigator or the subject, but not both, is unaware of whether active or control therapy is being administered. In double blind trials both the investigators and the participants are unaware of allocation to control study groups.

Confidence intervals — the confidence interval (CI) is the range of values for which the observed result is compatible, i.e. the confidence interval of a result from a study sample is the range of values in which it is fairly certain that the true population value lies (usually 95%). A range of possibilities for the population value is thus estimated, giving more useful information than merely classifying the result as 'significant' or 'non-significant'. If the confidence interval of the difference between treatments includes the value 0 then the study has failed to demonstrate a difference between the treatments, whereas if the value 0 is excluded from the confidence interval then a real difference is likely. Similarly, if the confidence intervals around a measure of an effect of two drugs overlap, then the study has failed to demonstrate a difference. On the other hand, if there is no overlap then a real difference is likely. More information can be gleaned by considering the width of confidence intervals.

Confounding — in any study the significance of association between variables or differences between groups may be undermined by the operation of factors, other than those under investigation, which may themselves explain part or all of the study's observations. Confounding occurs when an estimate of the association between an exposure and disease is mixed up with the real effect of another exposure on the same disease — two exposures are being correlated. Elimination of potential confounders is an important part of study design.

Correlation — when one variable changes in a defined way in relation to a second variable, the two are said to be correlated. Correlation implies an association, not causality. The correlation coefficient is a numerical expression of the strength and direction (positive or negative) of such an association.

Frequency distribution — this describes the way in which values within a given population are distributed. A normal distribution produces a uni-modal bell shaped curve in which 95% of the area under the curve lies within the range of the mean ±1.96 times the standard deviation and 99% of the area lies within the range of the mean ±2.58 times the standard deviation. When data is normally distributed, parametric statistical tests may be applied to them; when they are not, non-parametric statistics are used.

Incidence rate — the occurrence of new cases of a disease or condition within a specified population and period of time, e.g. the incidence of duodenal ulcer in the adult population is approximately 1% per year (compare with prevalence).

Intention to treat analysis — this is an analysis of the results in the control and treatment groups with respect to the number of patients entering the study, rather than those completing it. By including all entrants to the study, intention to treat analysis avoids biases due to failure of compliance and admits to side effects of therapy causing subjects to drop out from therapeutic trials. It provides an estimate of the overall benefit of therapy in the population studied.

Mean — average of a group of values.

Median — the middle score of a group of values, i.e. the value with equal numbers of other values above and below it.

Meta-analysis — a method of analysing data from more than one study, with the theoretical advantage of increasing sample sizes. Meta-analysis may detect differences which were not apparent with any confidence in individual studies with small sample sizes. Rigorous criteria for inclusion of data into meta-analyses must be applied to ensure that the data analysed are compatible.

Mode — the most frequently occurring value in a group of values.

Null hypothesis — this is an important concept in the design of trials and the understanding of probability. Tests of significance (hypothesis testing) are carried out to assess the probability that the observed differences between treatments could have arisen purely by chance and this is done by testing the results against a 'null hypothesis' of no true difference between treatments. The result of the test is expressed as a probability, the p value, of whether the observed data are consistent with the null hypothesis. By an arbitrary convention, a p value below 0.05 (which represents a 1 in 20 chance) is accepted as evidence of a true difference and is described as 'significant'. Conversely p values of 0.05 are regarded as being non-significant. This approach has two obvious drawbacks. Firstly, two values may be very similar e.g. $p = 0.051$ and $p = 0.049$ and although these are essentially similar values they would be regarded as non-significant and significant respectively. Secondly, significance tests give no indication of the magnitude of the observed difference between treatments, which would be more meaningful.

Odds ratio — this is the ratio of the odds of exposure among the cases, to the odds of exposure among the controls of a case-control study. It is a method of expressing risk reduction, see below for information on risk reduction measurements.

Power — power calculations involve the determination of sample sizes required to detect effect at the desired level of significance.

Predictive value — in evaluating a diagnostic test (e.g. screening) the positive predictive value is the probability of the person having the disease when the test is positive and the negative predictive value is the probability of the person not having the disease when the test is negative. Predictive value depends on the sensitivity and specificity of the test and, more importantly, on the prevalence of the disease in the population being tested.

Prevalence — the proportion of cases within a specified population at a given time (compare with incidence).

Risk reduction measurements — some clinical trials are carried out to test the effect of preventative therapy on the risk of experiencing an adverse event, and the method of describing differences in risk reduction has been shown to affect how such differences are perceived. Study results are often presented in terms of the relative risk reduction but this may give the reader a misleading impression of the actual magnitude of the benefit therapy since it does not indicate the underlying incidence of an event being prevented. The relative risk is a ratio of the incidence of disease in exposed persons to the incidence in non-exposed persons. A more useful expression of results is the NNT (number needed to treat). This is the number of patients who would need to be treated to prevent one clinical event and it is the reciprocal of the absolute risk reduction. Thus results are put in a more meaningful context, enabling comparisons between different interventions to be made. For example, the reduction in relative risk may be the same but the number needed to treat may be 20 patients in one example and 200 in another.

Sensitivity and specificity — these are terms applied to a diagnostic test, such as a screening test. A screening test must be reliable, providing consistent results, and valid, correctly categorising people into groups with or without disease. Sensitivity is the proportion of truly ill people in the screened population who are identified as ill by the screening test (probability of a positive test in people with the disease) and specificity is the proportion of truly healthy people who are so identified by the screening test (probability of a negative test in people without the disease).

Stratification — a sampling method in which individuals for study are selected from within sub-groups of a population rather than sampling from the entire population. Stratification is carried out to ensure representiveness or to exclude bias.

Type 1 error — the error, in the analysis of data, of stating that a difference or effect is present when in fact it is not. Conventionally a numerical value is often set at 0.05, i.e. on 5% of occasions the size of difference found could have occurred entirely by chance.

Type 2 error — the error, in the analysis of data, of concluding that a difference or effect is not present when in fact it is — this is particularly important when sample sizes are small.

PRACTICE CRITICAL APPRAISAL QUESTIONS

(A) The following four papers show the range of research papers that can appear in journals. The papers include a randomised trial, a cohort study, a cross-sectional survey and a case-control study. Each study method has specific reasons for its use, according to the strength of evidence it presents as well as how it is interpreted and what precautions are needed in interpretation.

The principles applying to these sample questions provide important practice on Critical Appraisal. The MRCGP question format however may vary to reflect current emphasis within the exam. In your answer, restrict yourself to answering the question, and avoid widening the discussion to related topics unless asked to do so. Remember that the exercise is to see how well you can interpret a paper and understand its conclusions. In any paper, there are good and bad points contributing to how reliable and valid the interpretation is. In your answer use these points to justify your views on the strengths (and weaknesses) of the paper.

Critically appraise this article, focusing on the strengths and weaknesses of the study.

Paper reference: Sonke GS et al. Comparison of case fatality in smokers and non-smokers after acute cardiac event; *BMJ* 1997; 315: 992—3

Comparison of case fatality in smokers and non-smokers after acute cardiac event

Gabe S Sonke, Alistair W Stewart, Robert Beaglehole, Rod Jackson, Harvey D White.
Reprinted with the kind permission of the *British Medical Journal.*

Although smoking is a major modifiable risk factor for acute myocardial infarction, it has also been associated with an up to twofold lower risk of dying in hospital after an acute myocardial infarction.[1][2] We analysed data from a community based register of coronary heart disease to determine whether differences in case fatality (the proportion of those dying) between smokers and non-smokers are restricted to patients who have been admitted to hospital and to evaluate possible explanations for this smoker's paradox.

Subjects, methods and results

All deaths related to coronary causes and all admitted patients aged 25-64 who met predefined criteria for myocardial infarction or coronary death were identified in Auckland, New Zealand between 1986 and 1992 as part of the World Health Organisation MONICA (monitoring trends and determinants in cardiovascular disease) project. Study criteria, and methods of case finding and data collection procedures have been published.[3][4] Postmortem examinations were performed on 63% of those who died from cardiac causes. Deaths before admission to hospital, deaths within 28 days after admission, and the total number of deaths were measured. Smoking was determined by direct questioning of surviving patients and of relatives of those who died. Patients were classed as current smokers (those who smoked at least one cigarette a week at the onset of symptoms or gave up smoking less than one month before the index event), ex-smokers (those who had abstained from smoking for at least one month before the onset of symptoms) or non-smokers (those who had never smoked). Logistic regression models were used to assess the effects of smoking on case fatality after adjusting for age, sex, history of myocardial infarction and history of angina. For those admitted to hospital, adjustments were based on whether they received thrombolytic treatment. An adjustment for the year of infarction was included to account for time trends in event rates.

Between January 1986 and December 1992, 5106 patients with a definite myocardial infarction or who died from coronary causes were identified. Of these, 2166 were current smokers, 1477 were ex-smokers and 1088 were non-smokers; information on smoking was missing for 375 patients, 231 of whom died before admission to hospital. Smokers were younger, more likely to be men, and fewer of them had a history of coronary heart disease when compared with non-smokers (table). The ex-smokers were older, more likely to be men, and more of them had previously had a myocardial infarction when compared with non-smokers.

Demographic information, case fatality, crude odds ratio and adjusted odds ratio by smoking status for acute cardiac events in patients aged 25-64 years, 1986-92

	Non-smokers (n=1,088)	Current smokers (n=2,166)	Ex-smokers (n=1,477)
Mean (SD) age (years)	55.8 (7.2)	53.3 (8.2)	56.7 (6.6)
No. (%) men	801/1088 (73.6)	1689/2166 (78.0)	1229/1477 (83.2)
No. (%) with previous myocardial infarction	257/1084 (23.7)	436/2153 (20.2)	552/1475 (37.4)
No. (%) with previous angina	243/1086 (22.4)	342/2158 (15.8)	301/1476 (20.4)
Case fatality (%)			
Before admission to hospital:	409/1088 (37.6)	831/2166 (38.4)	503/1477 (34.0)
Crude odds ratio* (95% Cl) (n=4,731)	1.00	1.03 (0.89 to 1.20)	0.86 (0.73 to 1.01)
Adjusted odds ratio* (95% Cl)	1.00	1.09 (0.93 to 1.27)	0.79 (0.67 to 0.94)
After admission to hospital:	123/679 (18.1)	157/1335 (11.8)	197/974 (20.2)
Crude odds ratio* (95% Cl) (n=2,988)	1.00	0.60 (0.47 to 0.78)	1.13 (0.88 to 1.45)
Adjusted odds ratio* (95% Cl)	1.00	0.72 (0.55 to 0.95)	0.93 (0.71 to 1.22)
Total:	532/1088 (48.9)	988/2166 (45.6)	700/1477 (47.4)
Crude odds ratio* (95% Cl) (n=4,731)	1.00	0.88 (0.76 to 1.01)	0.94 (0.81 to 1.10)
Adjusted odds ratio* (95% Cl)	1.00	0.97 (0.84 to 1.13)	0.85 (0.72 to 1.00)

* Odds ratio is the estimated odds of dying relative to a non-smoker

Compared with non-smokers, smokers had a higher risk of dying before hospital admission but this was not significant. The risk of dying after hospital admission was significantly lower in smokers. Overall, there was no significant effect of smoking on total case fatality because smokers who die before admission have a bigger effect on total case fatality than smokers who survive to be admitted. Ex-smokers had lower risks of dying both before and after hospital admission, resulting in an overall reduction in case fatality when compared with non-smokers.

Comment

We found a lower case fatality within 28 days after an acute cardiac event for smokers who had been admitted to hospital when compared with non-smokers; there was a non-significant rise in case fatality before admission to hospital in smokers. The lower case fatality after hospital admission among smokers is balanced by an excess in the number of smokers who died before hospital admission. There was no overall effect of smoking on case fatality from an acute cardiac event.

Adjusting for confounding reduced the apparent beneficial effect of smoking shown in the crude analysis of deaths after admission and increased the magnitude of the detrimental effect of smoking in the analysis of deaths before admission. The apparent decrease in case fatality in smokers after an acute cardiac event is restricted to patients who have been admitted, and the smoker's paradox is largely explained by a greater case fatality before admission to hospital in smokers.

Funding:Health Research Council of New Zealand and the National Heart Foundation of New Zealand.

Conflict of interest: None.

1. Barbash GI, Reiner J, White HD, Wilcox RG, Armstrong PW, Sadowski Z, et al. Evaluation of paradoxic beneficial effects of smoking in patients receiving thrombolytic therapy for acute myocardial infarction: mechanism of the "smoker's paradox" from the GUSTO-I trial, with angiographic insights. *J Am College Cardiol* 1995;26:1222-9.
2. White HD. Lifting the smoke-screen: the enigma of better outcome in smokers after myocardial infarction. *Am J Cardiol* 1995;75:278-9.
3. Tunstall-Pedoe H. Kuulasmaa K, Amouyel P. Arveiler D, Rajakangas AM, Pajak A for the WHO MONICA Project. Myocardial infarction and coronary deaths in the World Health Organisation MONICA Project. Registration procedures, event rates and case-fatality rates in 38 populations from 21 countries in four continents. *Circulation* 1994;90:583-612.
4. Sonke GS, Beaglehole R, Stewart AW, Jackson R, Stewart FM. Sex differences in case fatality before and after admission to hospital after acute cardiac events: analysis of community based coronary heart disease register. *BMJ* 1996;313:853-5.

Strengths

- Clear aims: reduction of number of deaths in smokers/non-smokers after cardiac event. This is an important area of health education in reducing mortality from smoking
- Study type: case controlled study matching the risk of dying between smokers and non-smokers following an acute myocardial infarction
- Matching: study group of smokers is matched to a control group of non-smokers
- Group selection: it is a register based study looking at all patients in Auckland with coronary related deaths. This reduces bias with regard to case selection
- Size: large number of cases (5106)
- Control matching: the mean age and age standard deviation (SD) is similar in all three groups
- Endpoint: death is a well-defined specific endpoint
- Statistical analysis: a logistic regression model allows us to assess the importance of several variables simultaneously, in this case age, sex, previous heart disease and previous MI, thereby reducing the effect of confounding (the explanation of the apparent difference between the two groups is in fact due to another unmeasured factor)
- Method: study criteria, methods of case finding and data collection procedures have been published.

Weaknesses

- Case-control study: lies lower down in the hierarchy of evidence
- Case-control study: shows association and not causation, i.e. the study does not say smoking causes less deaths following an acute cardiac event, it merely suggests an association which could equally be explained by other means
- Relevance to my practice: do patients in Auckland New Zealand match my own patients in the UK, i.e. are the results applicable to my population?
- Socio-economic data: no mention of racial characteristics and other socio-economic characteristics
- Other risk factors: no mention of weight, blood pressure, and cholesterol which could equally be factors relating to cardiac death
- Control matching: the three groups are not evenly matched in all aspects. A 10% difference in numbers of men between non-smokers and ex-smokers, and a 25% difference in absolute numbers between those with angina and no angina
- Causation link: the study does not look at heart attack prevention, it merely looks at what happens following a heart attack and the risk of death. In other words, it is the heart attack that causes the case fatality, not the smoking
- Statistical analysis: the odds ratio confidence interval ranges from 0·93–1·27 (smokers versus non-smokers reaching hospital alive). The significance is not strong
- Statistical analysis: the overall adjusted odds ratio on case fatality all cross 1 (that of the non-smoker) implying the possibility of no significant difference in the three groups.

Critically appraise this article focusing on the strengths and weaknesses of the study.

Paper reference: Watkins J. Effectiveness of influenza vaccination policy at targeting patients at high risk of complications during winter 1994-5: cross sectional survey; *BMJ* 1997; 315: 1069—70

Effectiveness of influenza vaccination policy at targeting patients at high risk of complications during winter 1994-5: cross sectional survey

John Watkins.

Reprinted with the kind permission of the *British Medical Journal*.

Each year the chief medical officer writes to general practitioners and other health professionals reminding them of the need to identify and vaccinate patients at risk of the complications of influenza - that is people who have chronic heart, chest, or kidney disease; people who have diabetes; people who are immunocompromised owing to treatment or disease and people living in residential accommodation. Routine immunisation of elderly people is not recommended. Current data on the efficacy of influenza vaccine indicates that up to 70% of clinical cases could be prevented,[1][2] an important finding as in 1989, 26000 people, mostly elderly, or those recommended for vaccination, died in the United Kingdom from influenza and its complications.[3] That year there was a good antigenic match between the epidemic strain and the one used in the vaccine, yet only one third to one half of all patients who would have benefited from vaccination received it.[4] I investigated the implementation of current vaccine policy.

Subjects, methods and results

In September 1994, 64 general practices in the county of Gwent, with a registered population of 291908, took part in a study that entailed data collection from patients at the time of vaccination. Patients were asked their age, whether they suffered with any of the conditions for which influenza vaccination is recommended, and the method by which they came to receive vaccination. A numerical coding system was used to separate out each chronic disease and the method used to contact patients. Only practices that were computer linked to the health authority patient register were used, and this provided patient denominator data. Practices for which the authority held denominator data on chronic diseases were used to calculate uptake rates of vaccine in at risk groups. Statistical analysis was carried out with SPSS 6.0 for Windows.

For the 28433 doses of vaccine given in the 64 practices, information was submitted on 21001 patients (74%). Overall, the vaccine uptake rate was 97.4 doses/1000 patients (table), though individual practices showed wide variation (range 25/1000 to 275/1000). Uptake rates in specific at risk groups were calculated for the practices that had recorded all of their immunisations. Analysis showed that under half of those patients identified as high risk and recommended for vaccination received it: only 63% of patients with heart disease, 39% with diabetes, 41% with asthma, and only one in three of those over 75. One quarter of all doses were given to patients at low risk. The table shows that advice from general practitioners accounted for 40% of all those being vaccinated, most of the remainder resulting from self referral by patients on an annual basis or on advice from the practice nurse. Other health professionals, particularly hospital consultants, played an insignificant part in vaccine promotion. Under 4% of patients were recruited by pro-active methods such as telephone, letter, or a message on repeat prescriptions; 80% were recruited opportunistically. Poster campaigns had little influence in targeting those who would most benefit. There was no significant difference in uptake rates between practices according to whether they were training practices or fundholders, had more than two partners, or occupied cost-rent premises. There was also no relation with list size, though those practices with the highest vaccination rates had the highest uptake in those who would most benefit.

Comment

The methods used in this study tend to overestimate the uptake of influenza vaccine in patients with heart and respiratory disease because of denominator deficiencies - for example, in calculating the uptake rate in patients with respiratory disease, the denominator population was calculated using the number of patients with known asthma and did not include other chest complaints, which would lead towards an over-estimation. This study showed that personal advice from a general practitioner or practice nurse during the vaccination period was the greatest stimulus to vaccine uptake. There was little evidence of practices using vaccination registers to plan their vaccination programmes, and other health workers, though targeting risk groups correctly, did so too infrequently to make an impact.

Influenza is an important disease of major public health concern, with

Doses of influenza vaccine given to patients at high and low risk, showing relation with methods by which patients were contacted. Numbers in parentheses are percentages of total doses arising from that method of contact, unless stated otherwise

Contact method	Patients of all ages at high risk	Well patients <65 years at low risk	Well patients >65 years at low risk	Patients with other conditions not recommended for vaccination	Total doses given (% of total doses given to study population)
Advice from general practitioner	5,495 (64)	480 (5.6)	1,737 (20.2)	869 (10.1)	8,581 (40.9)
Repeat prescription	263 (35.9)	73 (10)	332 (45.3)	64 (8.7)	732 (3.5)
Practice clinic	59 (86.7)	0	5 (7.4)	4 (5.9)	68 (0.3)
Hospital consultant	42 (84)	1	1	6 (12)	50 (0.2)
Practice nurse	1,809 (58.5)	232 (7.5)	563 (18.2)	486 (15.7)	3,090(14.8)
Health visitor	48 (46.2)	4 (3.8)	50 (48)	2	104 (0.5)
District nurse	83 (53.5)	7 (4.5)	43 (27.7)	22 (14.2)	155 (0.7)
Postal reminder	77 (70.6)	3	28 (25.7)	1	109 (0.5)
Telephone reminder	54 (66.6)	9 (11.1)	8 (.9.8)	10 (12.3)	81 (0.4)
Poster in surgery	243 (38.6)	153 (24.3)	72 (11.4)	161 (25.6)	629 (3)
Awareness due to media	66 (34.5)	63 (33)	27 (14.1)	35 (18.3)	191 (0.9)
Receives vaccine each year	2,168 (40.9)	1,079 (20.3)	1,445 (27.2)	608 (11.5)	5,300 (25.2)
Other method	476 (24.9)	691 (36)	408 (21.3)	336 (17.5)	1,911 (9)
Total (% of total doses given to study population)	1,0883 (51.8)	2,795 (13.3)	4,719 (22.5)	2,604 (12.4)	21,001 (100)

an effective vaccine. The United Kingdom currently spends over £30m on influenza vaccination (derived from the drug tariff cost per dose for six million doses of vaccine given in the winter of the study), yet this merely covers the cost of vaccine and fails to deal with organisational issues. I have shown that the present system, which relies on the idiosyncratic behaviour of individuals with minimal central guidance, no mechanisms to ensure effective targeting of vulnerable groups and no link between re-numeration and performance, results in less than half of those who require vaccination receiving it, while half is given to people at low risk. This approach falls short of delivering an evidence based public health policy aimed at reducing the impact of one of the world's major killer disease, as shown during the winter of 1989-90.

I thank Amer Jamil and Kerry Ross Jones for help with data entry, and Professor Peter Ellwood for his help and advice during the study.

Funding: The study was made possible by a research grant from the Association for Influenza Monitoring and Surveillance.

Conflict of interest: None.

1   Foster DA, Tolma A, Furomoto-Dawson A, Phmit SE, Margulies JR, Arden NH, et al. Influenza vaccine effectiveness in preventing hospitalisation for pneumonia in the elderly.

Am J Epidemiol 1992;136:296-307.

2   Nichol KL, Margolis KL, Wuorenma J. Van Sternberg T. The efficacy and cost effectiveness of vaccination against influenza amongst elderly persons living in the community. *N Engl J Med* 1994;331:778-84.

3   Curwen M, Dunnell K, Ashley J, Hidden influenza deaths. *BMJ* 1990;300:896.

4   Kurinczuk JJ, Nicholson KG, Uptake of influenza vaccination by patients with serious cardiac disease. *BMJ* 1989;299:367.

Strengths

- Clear aims: influenza vaccination targeted at the 'at risk' groups
- Study importance: important area with high morbidity (26,000 people died in 1989). 70% of deaths could be prevented
- Study type: cross-sectional survey appropriate for aim of study. Such a study looks to see how things are now, at a given point in time. Data is collected at a single point in time
- Study groups: well accepted risk groups identified (those patients with heart, lung, kidney disease, diabetes and immunocompromised)
- Study size: large population studied.

Weaknesses

- Paper clarity: there is lack of clarity in the paper. Figures seem to be mentioned without reference to tables. The figures are presented as fact without reference to result data
- Non-responders: large non-response rate (26%)
- Results: large skew with possible non-parametric data. Large variation from practice to practice (uptake rate 25/1000 to 275/1000). The average uptake rate of 97.4/1000 shows that more practices are at the lower limit than the higher limit. Due to the large skew in practice response rate, potential spurious and misleading estimates of significance can occur. Interestingly, there is no mention of result significance
- Questionnaire setting: as the study was done in a general practice setting, it is not surprising that 40.9% of patients recorded that their vaccination was a result of advice given by their GP. May have had a different result from asking patients in a hospital setting
- Health authority data accuracy: data depends on practice database; notoriously unreliable. The chronic disease database held by the Health Authority only shows those patients with asthma, and not those with chronic chest disease hence an overestimate of influenza vaccine uptake due to denominator database problems
- Database source: unclear as to how many of the 64 practices were involved in the final study.

Critically appraise this article, focusing on the strengths and weaknesses of the study.

Paper reference: Ridsdale L et al; Feasibility and effects of nurse run clinics for patients with epilepsy in general practice: randomised controlled trial; *BMJ* 1997; 314: 120—2

Feasibility and effects of nurse run clinics for patients with epilepsy in general practice: randomised controlled trial

L Ridsdale, D Robins, C Cryer, H Williams.

Reprinted with the kind permission of the *British Medical Journal*.

Abstract

Objective: To test the feasibility and effect of nurse run epilepsy clinics in primary care.

Design: A randomised controlled trial of nurse run clinics versus "usual care."

Setting: Six general practices in the South Thames region.

Subjects: 251 patients aged over 15 years who were taking anti-epileptic drugs or had a diagnosis of epilepsy and an attack in the past two years who met specified inclusion criteria and had responded to a questionnaire.

Main outcome measures: Questionnaire responses and recording of key variables extracted from the clinical records before and after the intervention.

Results: 127 patients were randomised to a nurse run clinic, of whom 106 (83%) attended. The nurse wrote 28 letters to the general practitioners suggesting changes in epilepsy management. For this intervention group compared with the usual care group there was a highly significant improvement in the level of advice recorded as having been given on drug compliance, adverse drug effects, driving, alcohol intake, and self help groups.

Conclusions: Nurse run clinics for patients with epilepsy were feasible and well attended. Such clinics can significantly improve the level of advice and drug management recorded.

Introduction

Self help groups, such as the British Epilepsy Association, have identified unmet needs for information and counselling among patients with epilepsy.[1] Recognising the unmet needs of such patients, the National Society for Epilepsy adopted a model used for other chronic conditions (such as diabetes) of training nurses to help patients to manage their own condition.[2]

We evaluated the usual care provided to 251 patients with epilepsy in six general practices.[3][4] We found that the advice which their doctors viewed as important for self management had frequently not been provided or recorded in the patients' notes. We then aimed to test the feasibility and effect of setting up a nurse run clinic in each of the six practices. We aimed *(a)* to establish whether patients with epilepsy would be willing to attend nurse run clinics and whether this would lead to more advice and monitoring of anti-epileptic drugs and *(b)* to ascertain the effect of the clinics on recording of advice on specified topics related to epilepsy.

Patients and Methods

The patients were all aged over 15 years, either took anti-epileptic drugs or had had a diagnosis of epilepsy and an attack in the previous two years, met specified inclusion criteria and had responded to a questionnaire on their physical and psychological condition. (The method for identifying patients is described elsewhere.[3])

We extracted from patients' records information on advice recorded as having been given to the 251 patients on specified topics (see table 2); this was stage 1 of the study. The patients were then randomised either to intervention (n=127) or to "usual care" (n=124). Those in the intervention group were offered an appointment with a nurse with special training in epilepsy (DR) at what was called a neurology clinic; those in the usual care group received care from their general practitioner or specialist (the care is described elsewhere.[3])

The nurse run clinics took place at the patients' own practice. The first appointment was for 45 to 50 minutes. The nurse asked about the frequency of epilepsy attacks and how patients managed their drugs; she took a blood sample for determination of plasma concentration of the drug if the patient was taking phenytoin, phenobarbitone or carbamazepine and had not had the concentration determined in the past year. Individual concerns were discussed. She also gave advice on various medical and social aspects of epilepsy when appropriate, together with information leaflets. The nurse used a structured record card to record the advice she gave.

A second appointment lasting 15-20 minutes was offered three months later. At this visit drug concentrations and drug taking were reviewed and advice and support offered. The nurse again used a structured record card to record the advice she gave.

About three months after the second appointment participants were sent a second questionnaire and advice given was reassessed using data extraction forms (stage 2). t tests and χ^2 tests were used to make comparisons between respondents and non- respondents and between the intervention group and the group receiving usual care.

Table 1 Nurse's reported findings and proposals* for changes in drug management about which she wrote to general practitioners of 28 patients

Finding or proposal	No. of patients
Proposed referral to specialist (patient taking several drugs; poor control)	9
Proposed increased dose of anti-epileptic drugs	5
Found adverse effects from anti-epileptic drugs	4
Found mismatch between specialist advice and drug taken	3
Proposed decrease in total daily drug dose	3
Proposed clobazam before menstruation	3
Proposed reduction in frequency of drug taking (but no overall reduction)	3

*There was more than one finding or proposal for some patients

Results

Participation and response rates have been described previously.[3] We found no significant differences in the age, sex, or recency of seizure for the two groups. Of the 127 patients offered a first appointment with the specialist nurse, 106 (83%) attended. No significant difference was found between patients who did and did not attend in terms of age (52.1 years v 48.5 years respectively, P=0.782) and sex (54.7% v 52.4% male, P=0.849). When offered a second appointment, 97/106 (92%) patients attended; 97/127 (76%) patients therefore attended both appointments. Between stage 1 and stage 2, 11 patients moved away, three died, and two were withdrawn by general practitioners or carers because of illness that met the exclusion criteria, leaving 235 patients in the study.

Drug management
At the start of the study 169/251 (67%) of patients were taking only one drug for their epilepsy. During the six months before stage 1, 36/127 (29%) of patients randomised to nurse run clinics and 29/124 (23%) of patients randomised to usual care had had their blood concentration checked (P=0.28). By stage 2, 80/121 (66%) of patients randomised to

nurse run clinics and 19/114 (17%) of patients randomised to usual care had had their blood concentration checked (P<0.01) in the previous six months. In some cases the nurse believed that the patient's drug management might be improved and she wrote 28 letters to patients' general practitioners about this (table 1).

Recording clinical advice before and after intervention

Clinical data were extracted from the notes of 232 out of the original 251 patients (119/127 in the intervention group and 113/124 in the usual care group) at stage 2. Table 2 shows the results according to intention to treat, which was the offer of appointments to see the nurse. The percentage of records with advice recorded as having been given on specified topics was not significantly different at stage 1 for the two groups. At stage 2 the percentage of records with advice recorded as having been given for each topic was significantly different (P<0.0001), with more information recorded as given in the group randomised to a nurse run clinic.

Discussion

This is the first report of a trial of the feasibility and effect of nurse run clinics for patients with epilepsy in general practice. We found that most patients with epilepsy were willing to attend a nurse run neurology clinic in primary care. The nurse was able to identify possible improvements in the drug management of over a fifth of the patients she saw. For the intervention group the level of advice recorded as having been given in the clinical records increased significantly. This needs to be interpreted cautiously as the nurse intervention was coupled with structured recording, which was likely to have had an additional effect.

This study was small in size and scope, focusing on process rather than outcomes. A larger sample size and longer intervention and follow up would be necessary to measure potential changes in medical outcomes. It may also be useful to develop an instrument to measure potential changes in patients' knowledge of their condition. The outcome in terms of patient satisfaction was independently assessed with quantitative and qualitative methods.

Table 2 Advice recorded as having been given to patients receiving usual care and to patients attending nurse run clinics. Values are numbers (percentages) of patients

Advice	Stage 1		Stage 2	
	Usual care (n=124)	Nurse run clinic (n=127)	Usual care (n=113)	Nurse run clinic (n=119)
Driving	57 (46)	59 (46)	52 (46)	84 (71)
Drug compliance	31 (25)	32 (25)	29 (26)	95 (80)
Adverse drug effects	10 (8)	13 (10)	18 (16)	86 (72)
Alcohol	13 (10)	15 (12)	16 (14)	92 (77)
Self-help groups	5 (4)	3 (2)	6 (5)	79 (66)

Members of the Evaluation Group comprised Drs. J. Close, A. Free, C. Hughes, Y. Hart, J. Ogden, A. Orme-Smith, N. Stoy and P. Stott.
We thank the British Epilepsy Association for providing free copies of their information leaflets and Professor Roger Jones for comments on a previous draft of the paper.
Funding: The Nuffield Provincial Hospitals Trust and the National Society for Epilepsy.

Conflict of interest: None

1. British Epilepsy Association. *Towards a new understanding.* Leeds: British Epilepsy Association 1990.
2. Shorvon SD, Dellaportas CI, Goodridge DMG, Bradbury C. *The clinical nurse specialist in epilepsy.* Chalfont St. Peter: National Society for Epilepsy, 1993.
3. Ridsdale L, Robins D, Fitzgerald A, Jeffery S, McGee L and the Epilepsy Care Evaluation Group. Epilepsy monitoring and advice: general practitioners' views, current practice and patients' preferences. *Br. J. Gen. Pract.* 1996;46:11-4.
4. Ridsdale L, Robins D, Fitzgerald A, Jeffery S, McGee L and the Epilepsy Care Evaluation Group. Epilepsy in general practice: patients' psychological symptoms and their perception of stigma. *Br. J. Gen. Pract.* 1996;46:365-6.

Strengths

- Clear aims: attendance, improving monitoring, and improving record keeping of advice
- Study criteria clearly defined: drug levels and management, advice, and recording of fit frequency
- Subject group defined: >15 years, +/- medication, epilepsy, inclusion criteria, answered questionnaire
- Study type: randomised control trial identifying a group of patients with epilepsy with a random allocation to intervention
- Group matching: equal numbers in two groups
- Group matching: no significant differences in age, sex or recentness of seizure
- Method: patient identification and usual GP care described in another paper
- Results: analysed by intention to treat, this avoids the problem of events happening to the study groups (drug dose alteration, treatment changes).

Weaknesses

- Study size: small
- Study group: the six practice demographics are not described. Are there equal numbers of patients in both arms of the study from each practice?
- Randomisation: no mention as to how the randomisation is achieved. Are all the patients randomised, or is the randomisation done within each practice?
- Nurse intervention: a nurse having 20—45 min to see one patient is not the same work pressure as a GP with average consultation rates. Comparability of the two study groups
- Study implications: the study looks at process rather than management. It treats record keeping as an indicator of epilepsy management. Do poor records mean poor management?
- Patient numbers: not all patients accounted for. Started with 251 patients, 16 patients accounted for in dropping out on entering stage 2 of trial, (235 patients) but data extracted in Table 2 add up to 232 patients, the missing patients being in the GP arm of the study
- Statistics: stage 2 of the trial looked at the data entered by the nurse in stage 1 of the trial. It is therefore not surprising that the records were more complete, i.e. the conclusion could have been anticipated. This is reported as highly significant ($p < 0.0001$) with more information recorded in the nurse-run clinic! The significance is meaningless in this context
- Study period: 3 months is short
- Outcome: medical outcome is not looked at, i.e. do the patients benefit medically over the long term with this extra input and time provided in the nurse-run clinic?

Critically appraise this article, focusing on the strengths and weaknesses of the study.

Paper reference: Gussekloo, R G et al. Impact of mild cognitive impairment on survival in very elderly people: cohort study; *BMJ* 1997; 315: 1053—4

Impact of mild cognitive impairment on survival in very elderly people: cohort study

J Gussekloo, R G J Westendorp, E J Remarque, A N Lagaay, T J Heeren, D L Knook.

Reprinted with the kind permission of the *British Medical Journal*.

Severe cognitive impairment is associated with increased mortality, but the impact of mild cognitive impairment on survival remains unclear.[1] [2] Although there is doubt whether a simple test such as the mini-mental state examination has sufficient discriminatory power to detect mild cognitive impairment in elderly people,[3] we determined the impact of borderline scores in this particular examination on survival in very elderly people.

Subjects, Methods and Results

As part of the Leiden 85-plus study[4] we followed a cohort of 891 subjects (641 women, 250 men) aged 85 years and over (median age 90 (range 85-103) years) from 1986 onwards. At entry to the study the score on the mini-mental state examination (Dutch version) was assessed by a physician during a home visit. In cooperation with the local government all but two subjects were followed for survival up to 1 October 1996. In all, 790 subjects died. Relative risks of mortality were estimated in a Cox proportional hazards model, which was adjusted for sex and age at baseline.

During the first year of follow up, the annual mortality risk for subjects with mild cognitive impairment (score 24-27 points, n=226) was twice as high (relative risk 1.8 (95% confidence interval 1.1 to 3.0)) as the annual mortality risk for subjects with a normal cognitive function (score 28-30 points, n=352). This difference in risk remained similar until the seventh year of follow-up, after which the annual mortality risk decreased to unity.

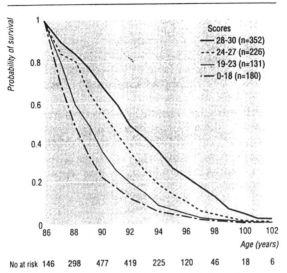

Survival probabilities from age of 86 years onwards for various categories of scores in the mini-mental state examination. Survival probabilities are calculated on data for 889 individuals followed for seven years, using actuarial method allowing individuals to enter survival table at different years of age (left censoring)

The cumulative mortality risk of the subjects with a mild cognitive impairment during the first seven years of follow up was 1.7 (1.4 to 2.0). This risk estimate was similar for men and women and for subjects below and over 90 years of age at baseline. Compared with subjects with a normal cognitive function, the cumulative mortality risk for subjects with a moderate cognitive impairment (score 19-23 points, n=131) was 2.5 (2.0 to 3.1) and for subjects with a severe cognitive impairment (score 0-18 points, n=180) the risk was 2.8 (2.3 to 3.4).

The association of scores in the mini-mental state examination and mortality is further illustrated in the figure representing the survival probabilities of subjects, calculated from the age of 86 years onwards.

Comment

In contrast with general belief, borderline scores in the mini-mental state examination cannot be considered to be normal and are associated with a significant decreased survival. Subjects with mild cognitive impairment may further deteriorate in cognitive function,[5] which is again associated with a lower survival.

It is not likely that all observed excess mortality is due to an effect of mild cognitive impairment. It may well be that milder cognitive impairments are associated with physical illness and disabilities, which could by themselves account for the decreased survival. A typical example is that atherosclerosis underlies decline of cognition, as well as cardiovascular disease. It is therefore difficult to determine which part of the observed mortality is due to atherosclerosis and which part to the mild impaired cognition.

Nevertheless borderline scores in the mini-mental state examination discriminate subjects with a higher risk of mortality. In practice, this easy to administer questionnaire seems to be useful as a screening instrument for mild cognitive impairment, and its scores may act as an important predictor of survival in very elderly people.

Funding: This study was partly funded by NIH (grant 5, RO 1 AG 06354) and by the Ministry of Health, Welfare and Sports.

Conflict of interest: None.

1. Kelman HR, Thomas C, Kennedy GJ, Cheng J. Cognitive impairment and mortality in older community residents. *Am J Public Health* 1994;84:1255-60.
2. Liu IY, LaCroix AZ, White LR, Kittner SJ, Wolf PA. Cognitive impairment and mortality: a study of possible confounders. *Am J Epidemiol* 1990;132:136-43.
3. Tombaugh TN, McIntyre NJ. The mini-mental state examination: a comprehensive review. *J Am Geriatr Soc* 1992;40:922-35.
4. Heeren TJ, Lagaay AM, van Beek WCA, Rooijmans HGM, Hijmans W. Reference values for the mini-mental state examination (MMSE) in octo- and nonagenarians. *J Am Geriatr Soc* 1990;38:1093-6.
5. Izaks GJ, Gussekloo J, Dermout KMT, Heeren TJ, Ligthart GJ. Three-year follow-up of mini-mental state examination score in community residents aged 85 and over. *Psychol Med* 1995;25:841-8.

Strengths

- Clear aims: mortality associated with mild cognitive impairment
- Study type: cohort study following patients through time to determine what happens to them. The design of the study is appropriate to the stated aims
- Study period: analysis is for an appropriate length of time (7 years) with the direction of time forward (i.e. not backwards as in a retrospective study)
- Bias reduction: the analysis has tried to balance the bias of age/sex difference by using a Cox proportional hazards model. The outcome (endpoint) of death is well defined and straightforward
- Control group: those with normal cognitive function are used for comparison, with reference to this control group
- Graph: well laid out and clear
- Study numbers: large
- Statistical results: the cumulative mortality risk during the first 7 years does appear to show a true difference with the mild (1.4—2), moderate (2—3.1) and severe (2.3—3.4) confidence intervals compared with normal cognitive function. There is overlap however in the moderate and severe group suggesting the significance may not be as strong in these areas.

Weaknesses

- Measurement: how accurate is mini-mental state questionnaire? Has it been validated to demonstrate levels of cognitive impairment? A full mental health questionnaire may have been more valid and powerful in defining the groups more precisely
- Patient source: not clearly defined — the only reference is the Leiden-85 plus study. How were these 891 patients identified?
- Confounding: when an observed relationship between two variables is due to the action of a third. In this case, the relationship of cognitive impairment and mortality may in fact be due to the action of a third (unaccounted for) variable such as disease. Other diseases that themselves are associated with cognitive impairment, such as cerebrovascular disease, may themselves lead to a decreased survival. In this example, it is the stroke that decreases survival rather than the reduced cognitive function
- Follow-up: no mention is made of any patients lost to follow up. Is this because the Leiden-85 group is already a pre-selected group and therefore open to bias?
- Interview technique: when patients are being interviewed, the nature of the questioning could influence the answers obtained. It is important that the questioner asks the questions in a standard manner and in a standard way
- Results: scoring system for cognitive impairment is not equal for all groups. The normal group had 3 scores (28—30), the mild group 4 scores (24—27), the moderate group 5 scores (19—23) and the severe group had 19 scores (0—18). How has mild been defined?
- Disease matching: this was not mentioned or allowed for between the groups.

(B) These questions are typical of those that you will be given in the MRCGP examination, mainly in Paper 1.

QUESTION 1

Your Practice Nurse approaches you and wants to set up a 'Healthy Heart Clinic' in the practice. She asks if you think the following study might be worth reading.

Paper reference: Baxter, T et al. A cost-effective community based heart health promotion project in England: prospective comparative study; *BMJ* 1997; 315: 582—5

(i)   List the strengths and weaknesses of the methodology in the abstract provided.
(ii) Basing your answer on this abstract briefly describe what advice you could offer as she reads the study herself.

A cost-effective, community based heart health promotion project in England: prospective comparative study

Tony Baxter, Philip Milner, Keith Wilson, Mike Leaf, Jon Nicholl, Nicola Cooper.

Reprinted with the kind permission of the *British Medical Journal*.

Introduction

Once established, coronary heart disease is impossible to cure, so a successful prevention strategy is the only way to reduce the long term burden.   Lifestyle risk factors are associated with the development of and mortality from coronary heart disease.[1-7] Prevention projects that focus on lifestyle risk factor modification have been shown to reduce the development of coronary heart disease and mortality from it.[8-11]

In 1991 we began a controlled, before and after study of the effects of a health promotion programme (Action Heart) using a population approach lasting four years to determine whether such an intervention was cost effective in a typical, non-teaching, English health district. The findings for children have been reported elsewhere.[12] We now report our findings in adults. Our objective was to evaluate the potential for producing lifestyle changes that affect the development of coronary heart disease.

Methods

The study design was a prospective, comparative study of the effects of the Action Heart health promotion intervention among two populations of adults. The intervention area, the adjacent communities of Swinton and Wath, was chosen for its high incidence of coronary heart disease. The control area (Maltby) had a similar record for coronary heart disease and socioeconomic composition (table 1). It was also sufficiently far from the intervention area to minimise contamination.

Action Heart used several recognised health promotion approaches[13] (see appendix 2 (http://www.bmj.com)).

Table 1 Standardised mortality ratios (SMR) from coronary heart disease in 1981-8 (95% confidence intervals) and rankings and values of electoral wards for deprivation indicators for control (Maltby) and intervention (Swinton and Wath) areas in 1990

Under 65 SMR 1981-1988	Maltby	Swinton	Wath
Men	138 (129 to 147)	131 (123 to 139)	136 (128 to 144)
Women	190 (184 to 196)	176 (171 to 181)	170 (165 to 175)
Deprivation rankings* (and values):			
Jarman score	14 (3.5)	12 (1.5)	9 (-1.2)
Department of the Environment index	13 (0)	11 (-0.6)	8 (-1.0)
Rotherham Metropolitan Borough Council index	16 (28)	9 (12.0)	13 (23.0)
Unemployment rate	12 (11.8)	10 (11.3)	7 (10.4)

*Among the 22 electoral wards in Rotherham

We assessed risk factor status using a self completed questionnaire covering personal details, sources of health information, personal history of blood pressure and cholesterol measurement, family health history, diet, exercise and smoking. Questions were chosen on the basis that they had previously been used in postal questionnaires; were free from bias and ambiguity; were appropriate for the Action Heart survey; had content validity; and were the subject of previous research.[14][15] The questions relating to smoking and milk consumption are shown in Appendix 1 (http://www.bmj.com).

At the time of sample size determination we did not know whether our study would receive funding and whether we could do a follow-up survey. However, we wanted to have good estimates of risk factor prevalence in the populations, while recognising that the sample size would be limited by the financial resources available. In undertaking sample size calculations based on confidence interval estimates, we assumed that *(a)* levels of risk factors in both areas were the same at baseline; *(b)* reductions in the level of cigarette smoking were the primary end point; *(c)* the prevalence of smoking in both areas was 34% at baseline; and *(d)* reductions over three years in the prevalence of cigarette smoking attributable to Action Heart which would be considered of public health importance were of the order of 2%.

To estimate smoking prevalence within 1% of the true value with 95% probability required an achieved sample size of 1509 from each area. To attain this, we mailed 1887 questionnaires to each area assuming an 80% response rate. We assumed that any background changes in smoking prevalence would be the same in both areas. The General Household Survey estimated that smoking prevalence was reducing by 1% per year in the age groups chosen.[16]

Questionnaires were mailed to a randomly chosen sample of named adults from the Rotherham Family Health Services Authority population age-sex register. The baseline survey was carried out in July 1991. The post-intervention survey was carried out in June 1995 using a similar approach but sent to a different random sample. (Following the cohort of individuals identified in the baseline survey would have increased statistical power but cost too much).

The proportions of questionnaires mailed to the subgroups of men or women aged 18-40 or 41-64 were the same in both intervention and control areas for the 1991 survey. In the 1995 survey the proportions of mailed questionnaires were adjusted to try to achieve equal numbers of respondents in each of the four age-sex subgroups based on the 1991 survey response rates. This ensured best estimates of risk factor prevalences in the subgroups. However, the response proportions for age-sex subgroups were not the same as those in the underlying population for both areas as measured by the 1991 and 1995 estimates from the Office of Population Censuses and Surveys modified by local authority estimates. To adjust for overcoverage and undercoverage in the four age-sex subgroups due to this sampling frame error[17] we weighted the responses so that they were directly proportional to the corresponding subgroups in the OPCS ward populations. Weighted data were used only in the univariate analysis. Age and gender terms were used in all of the logistic regression models.

Coding - Decision rules for coding to define outcomes were made by the senior registrar in public health and a research officer.

Analysis - A univariate analysis was used to compare the prevalence of lifestyle risk factors between the control and intervention communities from 1991 to 1995. The effect of the intervention on lifestyle behaviours was evaluated using multiple logistic regression to model the proportion with a particular behaviour in the study communities as a function of age-group (18-40 or 41-64), sex, the year of observation (1991 or 1995), and area (intervention or control). After modelling the prevalence of the lifestyle behaviours for sex, area and age group separately, the effect of the intervention was measured by comparing the change in the proportion showing that behaviour between 1991 (preintervention) and 1995 (postintervention) in the intervention area with the change between 1991 and 1995 in the control area, the test being based on the interaction between year and area. We also examined whether the effect of the intervention differed between the age groups and sexes.

Economics - A cost-effectiveness analysis was undertaken from the perspective of the purchaser, Rotherham Health Authority, to determine the technical efficiency of the Action Heart programme compared with traditional investment in disease management and other health promotion approaches to coronary heart disease. Outcomes were measured in units of life years gained, estimated from reported changes in smoking status using an epidemiological model. Cost data were collected in two ways. Firstly, data were extracted from financial records kept during the trial which listed actual expenditure over the four year study from a designated budget. Secondly, estimates of non-project staff costs and overheads incurred by the project were measured using diaries and timesheets kept by staff since the launch of Action Heart. Whitley Council pay scale rates were used to estimate the value of staff time. Costs relating to the research aspects of the trial were excluded from this analysis. Costs were discounted at the government recommended rate of 6%.[18]

SPECIMEN ANSWER SCHEDULE 1

(i)
Strengths

Design
- Community-based study in peer reviewed journal
- Prospective control design seems appropriate. Control group selection reasonable.

Questionnaire
- Seems thorough, and some evidence of prior reliability.

Intervention
- Details of programme readily available and 'recognised' approaches used.

Weaknesses

Sample
- Initial sample size calculated without follow-up survey even planned
- Are the assumptions made in calculating sample size valid? No justification of them
- Different cohort used in follow-up survey for financial reasons.

Risk factor assessment
- Self-reporting in questionnaire – likely bias and no objective tests employed
- Weighting process used to adjust for different age – sex subgroup responses.

Outcome
- Coding process not explicit
- Economic outcome measured in terms of mortality only (i.e. not morbidity)
- Analysis of changes in behaviour relies heavily on validity of projection models.

(ii)
Advice to the Nurse
- Find out how far the study group is representative of her practice
- Ascertain details of exactly what the intervention involved
- Try and identify from the results any *objective* changes achieved and whether these can reliably be converted into long term outcomes.

QUESTION 2

Mrs P is a 75-year-old lady who for years has taken frusemide 40 mg each morning for the control of ankle oedema. She asks you if she can stop these now.

Paper reference: Walma, E P et al. Withdrawal of long-term diuretic medication in elderly patients: a double-blind randomised trial; *BMJ* 1997; 315; 446—8

(i) List the strengths and weaknesses in the methodology of the study abstract included.

(ii) Comment on the advice you would give Mrs P based on the methodology and results shown.

Withdrawal of long term diuretic medication in elderly patients: a double blind randomised trial

Edmond P Walma, Arno W. Hoes, Colette van Dooren, Ad Prins, Emiel van der Does.
Reprinted with the kind permission of the *British Medical Journal.*

Introduction

Diuretics are among the most frequently prescribed drugs in Western societies, with about 20% of elderly patients using them long term.[1-3] Heart failure and hypertension are the major indications, and the cost-effectiveness of diuretics in these conditions is well established. Inappropriate prescribing, however, based on premature indications or uncritical repetitions of prescriptions, leads to unnecessary use of diuretics and should be minimised because of potentially serious side effects such as hypokalemia, hyponatriemia, dehydration, and cardiac arrest.[4-6] For the treatment of hypertension, dose reduction or cessation is generally recommended when blood pressures remain within normal limits over one to two years of treatment.[7 8] In heart failure new insights about the harmful long term effects of chronic activation of the renin-angiotensin-aldosterone system by diuretic therapy have led to an increasing number of recommendations to aim for the lowest possible dose of diuretics.[9-11] The possibility of withdrawing diuretic therapy in patients with heart failure but no signs of congestion has been studied in only one randomised trial, which replaced diuretics with angiotensin converting enzyme inhibitors.[12]

Primary care physicians account for most diuretic prescriptions.[1] We therefore performed a double blind randomised trial among elderly patients in general practice to assess what proportion could be successfully withdrawn from diuretic therapy.

Methods

Protocol

Patients aged 65 or more who had been receiving diuretics for at least six months and had no overt heart failure or hypertension were eligible for the trial. By scanning the pharmacy registers of eight general practices we identified 470 patients receiving long term diuretic therapy, of whom 268 were excluded because of a history of acute heart failure, defined as admission to hospital or prescription of intravenous diuretic therapy (27); symptoms of heart failure during the previous three months (21); manifest heart failure, defined as a heart failure score (see below) of over 4 (39); use of frusemide at dosages over 80 mg/day (26); mean of three blood pressure values (two measured at successive home visits and one obtained from the medical file) >180/100 mm Hg (21); hypercalciuria, nephrotic syndrome, and glaucoma (2); use of fixed combinations of diuretics with β blockers or angiotensin converting enzyme inhibitors (25); combination therapy of β blockers, diuretics, and vasodilators for hypertension (2); use of a diuretic for which no placebo was available (40); and non-compliance during the run-in phase (1). In addition, 57 patients or their general practitioners refused to cooperate and seven eligible patients could not be enrolled in the trial for logistic reasons.

Each general practitioner filled out a questionnaire to assess the patient's current indications for diuretic treatment. The sample size calculation was based on the assumption that a difference of 20% between the interventions was clinically relevant and a formula was used as given by Pocock.[13] The protocol was approved by the medical ethics committee of Erasmus University/Academic Hospital Dijkzigt Rotterdam and written informed consent was obtained from all patients.

Outcomes

The primary outcome variable was successful withdrawal from diuretic therapy. Patients in the withdrawal group who were still taking blinded study medication at the end of the six month follow up period were considered successfully withdrawn. Those patients who met one of the predefined criteria for requiring diuretic therapy within the follow-up period were considered to be unsuccessfully withdrawn. Criteria for prescription of diuretic therapy were: *(a)* heart failure score exceeding 4 points or *(b)* a mean of three duplicate systolic or diastolic blood pressure measurements on separate occasions of >180 mm Hg or >100 mm Hg respectively. Further, patients in whom diuretic therapy was restarted by their doctor for other reasons - for example, symptoms of increased shortness of breath - were considered to be unsuccessfully withdrawn. Changes in systolic and diastolic blood pressures are presented as secondary outcomes.

Baseline assessments and assignment
The run in phase of four weeks included two home visits (by EPW and CvD) to collect baseline data and perform the randomisation. At the first visit all diuretic medication was handed over to the research physician and replaced by active run in medication of the corresponding diuretic. At the second home visit, at the end of the run in phase, each patient was randomly assigned to placebo (the withdrawal group) or continuation of diuretic therapy (the control group), after stratification by age (65-79 and >80 years) and type of diuretic. Blocks of four sets of study medication each consisted of two placebo and two genuine packages, which were consecutively assigned to enrolled patients. Patients with frusemide dosages of 40 or 80 mg/day went through a dose halving regimen of one and two weeks, respectively, to prevent severe rebound effects. Dose halving was started immediately after randomisation and was performed double blind. Randomisation lists and numbered sets of study medication were generated by the trial pharmacist of the Academic Hospital, who also produced sealed envelopes with decoding information for emergencies.

Blinding procedure and drug compliance
Matching placebo was available for the five diuretics or fixed diuretic combinations most often prescribed in our region: frusemide, chlorothalidone, hydrochlorothiazide plus triamterene, epitizide plus triamterene, and triamterene, covering 90% of all diuretic use. The similarity of genuine and placebo tablets ensured the impossibility of recognising them by colour, form or taste. The randomisation list remained in the pharmacy of the Academic Hospital in Rotterdam, separate from the trial centre in Schoonhoven. Of the sealed envelopes one copy was kept in the trial centre and another with the patient at home (for emergencies). The codes were broken either after the assessment of the last set of data, or when a diuretic prescription was needed, in which case the primary outcome of the study became actual. This blinding

procedure was tested one month after randomisation by asking both the patient and the trial doctors their opinion about the content of the trial medication. Drug compliance was checked by counting tablets and asking patients about compliance at every follow up contact and by assessment of serum diuretic concentrations (with high pressure liquid chromatography and ultraviolet fluorescence for chlorothalidone, triamterene and frusemide) at the start and the end of the study.

Follow up

During follow up participants were visited six times at their homes by study physicians (EPW, CvD) - 2 days, 1 and 2 weeks and 1, 3 and 6 months after randomisation. Heart failure score and blood pressure were assessed at baseline and at all follow up visits. Heart failure symptoms were measured by means of a scoring list, including paroxysmal nocturnal dyspnoea in the preceding week (3 points); dyspnoea on exertion in the preceding week (2 points); raised jugular venous pressure (2 points); heart rate >100 beats/min (1 point); hepatojugular reflux (1 point); lower pulmonary crepitations (1 point); S3 gallop rhythm (1 point); two sided pitting ankle oedema (1 point); and hepatomegaly (1 point). This symptom score list was validated separately.[14]

During the study duplicate blood pressure readings were taken with an Omron HEM-403C oscillometric automatic device with the patient sitting.[15] The arm with the highest blood pressure was determined at the first session and used throughout for further measurements. An electrocardiogram was recorded at baseline.

Table 2 Patients meeting one of the predefined clinical criteria requiring reinitiation of diuretic therapy. Results are numbers of patients

Criterion	Withdrawal group (n=102)	Control group (n=100)	Risk difference (%) (95% CI)
All	50	13	36 (22 to 50)
Heart failure*	25	4	21 (11 to 31)
Hypertension*	9	5	4 (-3 to 11)
Subjective shortness of breath	6	0	6 (1 to 11)
Non-cardiac ankle oedema	4	1	3 (-1 to 8)
Miscellaneous clinical conditions	3	1	2 (-2 to 6)
Other	3	2	1 (-3 to 5)

*The reason for re-initiation was classified as heart failure if patients had heart failure scores >4 points and as hypertension if the mean value of three consecutive systolic or diastolic blood pressure measurements on different occasions was >180 mm Hg or >100 mm Hg respectively

SPECIMEN ANSWER SCHEDULE 2

(i)
Strengths

Design
- GP based study in reputable journal
- Ethically approved and with informed consent of patients
- Double blind study
- Compliance with drug use checked objectively with blood tests.

Sample
- Excluded patients with overt heart failure and/or hypertension.

Outcome
- Outcome well defined
- Follow up very thorough.

Weaknesses

Sample
- Is the assumption that a 20% difference in the two groups for significance a valid one?
- Is the heart failure score used validated in GP use? Includes some clinical measures that seem subjective and not GP orientated (JVP, S3 Gallop).

Lost data and bias
- How did they select the eight practices and why did 57 doctors refuse to participate? Possible introduction of bias
- Large number of albeit well defined exclusion criteria — is this realistic in practice?
- Foreign study — is this representative of UK practice?

(ii)
Recommendations to Mrs P

- About 50% of patients need to restart the diuretic for significant reasons (failure/hypertension)
- She would need intense follow up
- Most patients seem to restart the diuretic within 4 weeks — perhaps the drug should be tailed off more gradually
- All patients in this study took either placebo or active treatment — the placebo effect may be significant
- The recurrence of ankle oedema may not be a problem (confidence interval crosses zero).

QUESTION 3

Mr O, a 35-year-old radiographer, presents with palpitations and anxiety. You hear an innocent systolic murmur. He asks if he ought to have an echocardiogram "just to make sure everything is OK".

Paper reference: McDonald, IG et al. Opening Pandora's Box: the unpredictability of reassurance by a normal test result: *BMJ* 1996; 229–32.

(i) List the strengths and weaknesses of the study abstract in relation to Mr O's clinical situation.
(ii) Briefly state whether the results of this study would affect your management of Mr O.

Opening Pandora's box: the unpredictability of reassurance by a normal test result

I G McDonald, J Daly, V M Jelinek, F Panetta, J M Gutman.

Reprinted with the kind permission of the *British Medical Journal*.

Introduction

Reassurance of patients concerned about a possible health problem is perhaps the commonest clinical transaction of all. Clinicians and textbooks generally assume that reassurance must logically follow a clear and confident statement that no disease has been found. Failure of reassurance may then be ascribed to neurosis or labelled as abnormal illness behaviour.[1] The anxiety which remains can seriously impair quality of life and result in unnecessary re-investigations, which are a burden on both the patient and the healthcare system. Despite the manifest importance of patient reassurance there has been remarkably little empirical study. We investigated this issue on the assumption that "The scientific resolution of most problems in clinical medical management will come from analyses of events and observations that occur in non-experimental circumstances during the interaction of nature, people, technological artefacts and clinical practitioners."[2]

Study population and methods

Six cardiologists in private practice and with university affiliation were each asked to recruit 10 consecutive patients who were referred to one of three laboratories (one public, two private) for the exclusion of heart disease. No cardiologist refused. Three recruited patients as requested and the remainder provided 10 patients between them. The sample of 40 patients recruited was sufficient to allow analysis in each major data category according to the principle of theoretical sampling.[3] Twenty-five patients were female and 15 male, and their average age was 32 years (range 3-74).

The symptomatic group (10 patients) presented because they were worried by symptoms, usually palpitations or chest pain or both. In the incidental group (30 patients) referral was for assessment of a systolic murmur detected during a routine examination in primary care (21 patients) or in the course of a pre-employment or insurance check (nine patients). A systolic murmur had been heard in 36 patients. Doubt had previously been raised about the heart in 13 patients - in one no fewer than four times - and echocardiography had been performed previously in six. Three patients had previously taken medication for the heart.

Data acquisition and analysis

Data analysed consisted of medical records, transcripts of tape recordings of the medical consultation in which the cardiologist had explained the test result, structured interviews with the cardiologists and semi-structured patient interviews.

The *cardiologist interview*, conducted by a consultant cardiologist, utilised a questionnaire developed for a previous study.[4] Data recorded included the reason for ordering the test, plans for patient management and gradings of perceived patient anxiety before and after the test. The pre test likelihood of cardiac normality was expressed as a grading on an ordinal scale of probabilities developed by a consensus method for the earlier study,[4] in which "probable" represented a subjective probability estimate between 0.65 and 0.89, "almost certain" a subjective probability estimate between 0.90 and 0.99 and "certain" a subjective probability estimate of more than 0.99. Patients were interviewed twice by a sociologist.

Patient interviews - The initial home interview was conducted as soon as possible after the medical consultation in which the test result had been explained (average 6.3 days). The follow up home interview, conducted nine to 12 months later, concentrated on subsequent progress and related medical events. One patient could not be located for the initial interview. Four patients were unavailable for follow up; all had changed address (one had moved interstate, one overseas).

These home interviews, roughly two hours long, were structured along the lines of routine medical history taking. Thus patients were encouraged to give a free account of their perceptions and problems and leading questions were kept to a minimum to ensure that the issues discussed were those of most concern to the patient. A short check list of direct questions, introduced as necessary at the end of the interview, was analogous to the clinical review of systems.

Analysis of transcripts - The protocol used for analysis of transcripts drew on an earlier study of patient responses.[5] Definitions of study variables and of the criteria used for their classification and grading have been reported.[6] So too have the details of the method and the results of qualitative analysis of the data.[7]

Grading quality of consultation - For the clinical consultations the important issues were what the cardiologist actually told the patient and generation of a grading of the quality of the consultation. An aggregate score was constructed as follows. A consultation was graded as "good" if *(a)* explicit information about the heart was stated clearly and with confidence, *(b)* the patient was provided with clear and persuasive reasons for the query and referral, and *(c)* the patient's views were elicited and discussed. The grading was "fair" if criterion *(a)* was met plus either *(b)* or *(c)*. In all other cases the grading was "poor".

Patient recall and understanding - At issue in the initial patient home interview were the accuracy of the patient's recall of what the cardiologist had said, level of understanding concerning the normality of the heart, and evidence of anxiety related to doubt or misunderstanding. Patient recall of the consultation was compared with what the cardiologist had actually said according to the transcript. From the patient's own account we graded pretest understanding as a composite index taking account of *(a)* understanding of the reason for the heart query and *(b)* understanding of the fact that serious disease was possible but unlikely. Post-test understanding was graded with respect to *(a)* understanding of the nature of the presenting symptoms or murmur and *(b)* appropriate acceptance that the heart was normal and the consequent implications for health. We graded the level of patient anxiety both before the test and after explanation of the normal result.

Observer agreement determined by comparison of the independent gradings made by a cardiologist (IMcD) and a sociologist (JD) has been presented in detail elsewhere.[6] Differences in mean observer gradings were not significant at the 5% level for any variable (Mann-Whitney U test).[8] When results for all four level grading scales were pooled there was complete agreement between observers[9] for 75.0% of gradings, minor disagreement (one grade) for 17.4% and serious disagreement (two grades) for 7.7% (Cohen's weighted κ 0.78; 95% confidence interval 0.73 to 0.81).[10] Agreement was therefore deemed to be satisfactory for 92.3% of gradings. Having documented the reproducibility of our application of the study protocol, the cardiologist and sociologist then graded each variable by consensus using direct quotations from the transcripts as supporting evidence. Of a total of 106 variables measured in the original study, consensus could not be reached on two, which were then eliminated from the study.

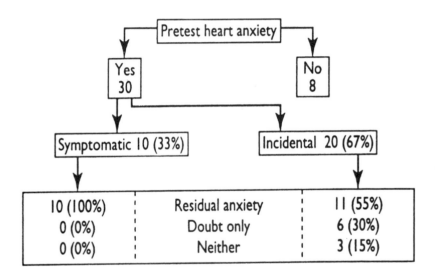

Fig 1. - *Patient's responses to test (echocardiogram) and explanation of normal result*

SPECIMEN ANSWER SCHEDULE 3

(i)
Strengths

Sample
- Age range relevant
- Clinical scenario fits, i.e. sample includes patients with normal hearts, functional murmurs and cardiac symptoms.

Assessment tool
- Made assessments of possible inter- and intra- observer bias.

Weaknesses

Sample
- Seems small despite statistical comments
- Is this the most appropriate study design? Absence of control group is a particular problem.

Lost data and bias
- Private practice patients from a university setting in secondary or even tertiary care
- Consecutive selection may introduce bias (may be a particular sort of specialist session)
- 10% patients lost to follow up
- Did the study process increase anxiety? Possible contamination of results.

Assessment tools
- Was the system for analysing consultation quality validated? It seems basic
- How was patient anxiety measured? Could this have been more blinded?
- A single observer used in the cardiologist interview — intra-observer error possible. This was checked — 'minor' or more significant disagreement 'in 25% of gradings'. What does this mean? Who defined the major/minor scale? Suggests inter-observer variation and reduced reliability of assessments
- Not clear how many interviewers conducted home assessments - possible inter-observer bias. Why was more than one used?

Follow up
- Patients seen as soon as possible after interview — but actually at an *average* of 6 days. If the aim was as soon as possible why the delay?
- Follow up for 9—12 months — does anxiety settle with time? No check on this or any other factors that may have been relevant.

(ii)
Management of Mr. O.

This study probably has little relevance to general practice. The success of reassurance is likely to lie within 'category (c)' listed in the method, i.e. eliciting and discussing the patient's views. The results show 100% of symptomatic (10/10) patients had residual anxiety but do not relate this to the 'quality' of the consultation. A test on its own is not helpful and that is perhaps not surprising.

Overall:
1 Study of little help to GP
2 Quality of consultation is the probable key
3 Tests applied with simple reassurance are probably unhelpful.

QUESTION 4

You are writing a protocol for minor surgery in your practice. You are considering the proposal that all specimens removed should be sent for histology.

Paper reference: Lowy A et al. Is histological examination of tissue removed by general practitioners always necessary? Before and after comparison of detection rates of serious illnesses; *BMJ* 1997; 315: 406—8.

(i)   List the strengths and weaknesses of the study abstract relevant to your consideration.
(ii) Explain, with justification, which points of this study you think should influence your protocol design.

Is histological examination of tissue removed by general practitioners always necessary? Before and after comparison of detection rates of serious skin lesions

Adam Lowy, Diane Willis, Keith Abrams.

Introduction

Since the changes to general practitioners' contracts in 1990[1] the volume of minor surgery by general practitioners has increased substantially.[2] Around 40% of lesions excised by general practitioners are not referred to a pathologist.[3][4] Several researchers have reported diagnostic errors and incomplete excision of malignant lesions by general practitioners[5-9] and have recommended mandatory pathological examination, a proposal supported by the Royal College of General Practitioners and other professional bodies.[10]

Whether this policy would benefit patients is unclear. Research has been restricted to specimens that general practitioners have chosen to send, undoubtedly introducing a bias towards "problematic" lesions. Nothing is known about the histological nature of lesions that general practitioners discard. Most are clinically diagnosed as ingrown toenails, foreign bodies, skin tags, warts, ganglia, cysts and other benign lesions,[4] so it is possible that a few serious lesions are currently discarded. Although histological examination cannot harm the patient and might help, this alone does not necessarily constitute grounds for investigation, a principle that is widely accepted in other areas of clinical practice (*x* ray examinations, for example, are not automatically performed after head injury[11] or ankle inversion[12] because this approach is acknowledged to result in wasteful overinvestigation). Paraskevopoulos and colleagues questioned the need to examine all tissue excised during minor operations in hospital, concluding that the risks of missing an important diagnosis seemed exceptionally small for what appeared to be a considerable saving in time and money.[13]

General practitioners probably discard about 250000 excision specimens annually;[4] at about £18 each[3] it would cost £4.5m a year to examine them all. The Royal College of Pathologists recommends that a consultant pathologist examines 2000-3000 surgical specimens a year.[14] Although specimens from minor surgery are often straightforward to examine, Paraskevopoulos and colleagues suggest that 5000 such specimens would represent a year's work for a consultant.[13] It is not known whether the benefits of examining histologically the specimens that general practitioners discard would outweigh the cost in pathologists' time (or indeed whether any benefit would result),[15] and we examined what the impact of such a policy would be.

Methods

We randomly selected 24 pathology laboratories in England.[16] Three pathologists refused to take part, one because of impending retirement and two because of concern about workload. We also randomly selected, in the catchment area of each laboratory, 8-18 general practitioner partnerships offering minor surgery. Partnerships were excluded if they performed fewer than four excisions a month or if they had merged or split, changed the number of partners, or extended or restricted their provision of minor surgery since September 1991 (or anticipated doing so before the end of the study).

The practices agreed to obtain a histological diagnosis from their usual laboratory on all solid tissue removed by any minor surgery (including cautery and diathermy) from 1 September 1993 to 28 February 1994. Histological diagnosis, date of surgery, and practice code were collected from pathology reports for all specimens sent by the practices during the intervention period and during a 6 month control period (1 September 1992 to 28 February 1993) before the intervention.

Two of the 21 areas were excluded because of problems with their databases. The effects of the intervention were estimated as differences in incidence; when we found evidence against a uniform intervention effect this was taken account of in stratified random-effect analyses.

Results

Of 330 partnerships in the 19 areas, 257 (response rate 78%) took part (914 general practitioners, 1.6 million person years and 10153 specimens). The overall referral rate increased by 29% (table 1). Although the impact on referral rates varied significantly between the areas ($\chi^2 = 162$, df=18, P<0.001), this appeared to be due simply to the large variation between practices, rather than to a true area effect. A random-effect analysis, in which the underlying intervention effect was considered to vary between practices, showed an average increase in referrals of 1.34 specimens per 1000 person years (95% confidence interval 0.93 to 1.76).

The impact of the intervention on the detection of malignant and premalignant lesions was negligible (table 2), with the small falls in malignant lesions probably being the result of chance. The bulk of the increased number of referrals comprised viral warts, seborrhoeic keratoses, and ingrown toenails (1729 in the control period, 2886 during the intervention; difference in detection rate 1.4 lesions per 1000 person years (95% confidence interval 1.3 to 1.6 P<0.001)); the increase in other benign lesions was smaller (2409 v 2720; 0.38 (0.21 to 0.56, P<0.001))

Table 1 Referral rates of tissue specimens sent by general practitioners in intervention and control periods

Period	No. of specimens referred	Rate per 1000 person years	Adjusted rate difference (95% CI)
Control period	4430	5.49	1.34 per 1000 person years
Intervention period	5723	7.08	(0.93 to 1.76)*

* P<0.001

Table 2 Malignant and premalignant skin lesions detected in control and intervention periods

Type of lesion	Control period	Intervention period	Detection rate difference (lesions/million person years 95% CI)
Pre-malignant lesions	91	98	9 (-25 to 42)
Malignant lesions:	204	188	-20 (-68 to 28)
Non-melanoma malignancy	188	173	-18.6 (-65 to 28)
Malignant melanoma	16	15	-1.2 (-15 to 12)
Malignant and pre-malignant lesions	295	286	-11.1 (-70 to 47)

SPECIMEN ANSWER SCHEDULE 4

(i)
Strengths

Design
• Very large random sample.

Data collection
• Fairly good response rate (78%).

Weaknesses

Design
- Was 6 months a suitable study period? Natural variations in number of samples may hide any intervention effect. A longer time period may even this effect out.

Lost data
- 3/24 pathologists refused to take part — possible bias
- Why exclude partnerships with low numbers? — may be that this is the most important group to study
- Why exclude merged/split practices or ones that had extended/ restricted services since 1991? — possible distortion of results
- 2/21 had 'problems with their database'. Why? Possible bias introduced by this 10% loss of data.

(ii)
Points that would influence protocol

- Sending all specimens increases referral rates by 29% **BUT:** this actually means only about two extra specimens per GP per year
- Wide confidence intervals in Table 2 make extrapolation from the results difficult — suggests the sample was too small
- Detection rates of malignancies were not influenced by the intervention
- A large proportion of the increase in samples sent for histology was warts/toenails i.e. lesions where there is no suggestion of malignancy.

It would seem that sending all samples as a blanket rule is not necessary — it would increase laboratory workload with no clinical benefit.

QUESTION 5

A practice protocol stipulates that all patients suffering from atrial fibrillation who have no contra-indications should be on aspirin or anti-coagulants.

An audit of anti-thrombolytic therapy in the practice (list size 6,000) produced the following data:

- 11 patients were on aspirin
- 9 were on warfarin
- 10 were on neither.

Comment on the results under the following headings:

(i)   audit criteria
(ii) quality of data
(iii) clinical interpretation
(iv) policy implications

SPECIMEN ANSWER SCHEDULE 5

(i) Audit criteria

- Rationale — how have the criteria been established?
- What contra-indications to anti-thrombosis therapy have been decided and on what evidence?
- Standard settings — what is the gold standard?

(ii) Quality of data

- Sampling — is the database correct?
- How was the data affected? Computer records?
- Repeat prescriptions.

(iii) Clinical interpretation

- Limited — small numbers, flawed methodology
- Audit standards — was the gold standard reached? Was the standard set reasonable? i.e. should it have been lower in the first instance?
- Explanation. Why 10 patients on neither aspirin or warfarin?

(iv) Policy implications

- Protocol — should this be changed — expert input? Data recordings — is this sufficient? How can it be improved? e.g. Recording from specialists letters; all partners checking information is properly recorded on the computer when patient seen
- Raising awareness in the practice that patients with atrial fibrillation should be on anti-thrombolytic therapy. Practice meeting; review of literature
- Re-audit — when and with what modification to criteria and standards
- Costs — what are the costs in terms of time and outgoing for this task
- Practice changes — what changes should take place as a result of this audit? e.g. improved data collection, education of doctors, practice nurses in over 75 checks
- Staff — involvement of practice manager and practice nurses.

QUESTION 6

A six partner seaside general practice reviews its prescribing costs. The following data were obtained.

The comparative costs of the various drugs used by temporary residents (TR) as opposed to the practice's own patients.

	Cost per own patient (£)	Cost per TR (£)
GIT drugs	1.56	0.30
cardiovascular drugs	1.58	0.25
respiratory drugs	1.01	0.21
CNS drugs	1.02	0.18
anti-infectives	0.54	1.59
endocrine drugs	0.62	0.14
joint disease drugs	0.83	0.20
skin preparations	0.41	0.78
vaccines	0.03	0.04
dressings	0.23	0.17

Comment on the data, giving possible explanations for your observations.

SPECIMEN ANSWER SCHEDULE 6

- Lowered costs per patient noted for TR in all areas except anti-infectives, skin preparations and vaccines, with only slight reduction in dressings
- It is not stated if the average cost is over the whole year or just one quarter. Possibly only over busy summer quarter when there is an influx of seaside visitors.

- **Factors in Patients**

a)   Increased TR costs

Increased infections, especially minor, e.g. URTI. In considering increased vaccines and only slightly reduced dressings costs, possibility of increased wound infections, receiving tetanus booster and dressings. Increase in minor skin disorders, especially sunburn or skin irritations.

b)   Reduced TR costs

Little long-term prescribing for major prescribing areas, especially CNS. Possibly reflects younger population of visitors and that they obtained long-term medications from their own GP prior to visiting area.

- **Factors in Doctors**

a)   Possibly little patient education (altering patients' health beliefs and health-seeking behaviour) for minor infections and skin irritations.

b)   'Symptom' prescribing for minor problems, related to TR patient expectations, volume of workload, patients' psycho-social factors and whether seen at surgery or at home visit.

QUESTION 7

Comment on the presented data, giving possible explanations for your observations.

GP direct access physiotherapy service		
Number of referrals received		176
Total number of patients seen		157
Number	Failed first appointment	31
	Unable to attend	47
	Did not attend	16

Signed
Head of Physiotherapy
Community Physiotherapy Service

SPECIMEN ANSWER SCHEDULE 7

- The presented data and the table were unclear.

a) 'Failed first appointment' and 'did not attend' amalgamated to produce 'unable to attend' or are all 3 categories separate?

b) How are the categories 'failed first appointment', 'unable to attend' and 'did not attend' distinguished?

c) Whatever combination is considered, they do not reflect the difference between 'number of referrals received' and 'total number of patients seen'.

- Approximately 11% of referrals made are not seen. This does not seem to be unreasonable, but there are wasted appointments
- Failure to attend first appointment may be due to several factors e.g. long waiting list, with resolution of problem or seeking of alternative private referral, inconvenient time or date
- Further information on the categories is essential before meaningful conclusions can be made.

QUESTION 8

Catheter care — practice protocol

Long term catheters are associated with a number of complications — blockage, bypassing, stone formation and periurethral abscesses. These may be minimised by correct care.

- Avoid kinking of drainage tube
- Avoid constipation, regular laxatives will help
- Maintain a high fluid intake
- Arrange plain abdominal X-ray if bladder stone is suspected — refer if confirmed
- Ascorbic acid 1 G t.d.s. acidifies urine and may decrease stone formation
- Bendrofluazide 5 mg nocte will decrease phosphate encrustation
- Bladder washouts do little to help and should be avoided
- If bypassing is a problem ensure catheter is not blocked, try probanthine 15 mg t.d.s. If problem persists a suprapubic catheter may be the answer — refer for this
- Periurethral abscesses require antibiotics and possibly admission and drainage if the patient is ill.

You are presented with this protocol. List recommendations for improving the protocol, giving your reasons.

SPECIMEN ANSWER SCHEDULE 8

Recommendations for improvements

Purpose and scope
- Clear description of patient group to whom it will apply and the health care providers who will be applying it e.g. age and sex range
- Identification of who is responsible for the development of the protocol e.g. primary or secondary care/medical or nursing staff.

Clinical flexibility
- Specific information about situations in which clinical exceptions might be made on applying the protocol e.g. spinal injuries or after stroke.

Validity
- Specific description of methods used to collect the evidence on which the recommendations in the protocol are based
- Adequate supporting references
- Are they evidence based?
- Are they mere anecdote?
- Comparison with other guidelines, protocols or expert reviews.

Multidisciplinary process
- Clear description of who participated in the development of the protocol
- Any potential biases should be noted e.g. commercial sponsorship.

Likely cost and benefits
- Discussion of both financial and patient cost-benefit outcomes for the recommendations.

Clarity
- Need for clear and unambiguous presentation.

Clinical audit
- Should state specific criteria for monitoring compliance of protocol.

Review and updating
- Specific date for reviewing or updating stated
- Description of who will be responsible and how it will be reviewed or updated.

QUESTION 9

Use of dipstick haematuria in the detection of carcinoma of the bladder

A practice screens 459 men between 60 and 80 years with dipstick for haematuria, referring any positive results for urological investigation.

	Disease status	
	Carcinoma of bladder	No carcinoma of bladder detected
Dipstick positive	4	8
Dipstick negative	1	446

What is the sensitivity and specificity and positive predictive value of this test?

SPECIMEN ANSWER SCHEDULE 9

Sensitivity
Possibility of a positive test in people with disease

$$\frac{\text{Number of true positives}}{\text{Number of true positives} + \text{number of false negatives}}$$

$$\frac{4}{4+1} = 80\%$$

Specificity
Probability of a negative test in people without the disease

$$\frac{\text{Number of true negatives}}{\text{Number of false positives} + \text{number of true negatives}}$$

$$\frac{446}{8+446} = 98\%$$

Positive predictive value
Probability of the person having the disease when the test is value positive

$$\frac{\text{Number of true positives}}{\text{Number of true positives} + \text{number of false positives}}$$

$$\frac{4}{4+8} = 33\%$$

This is low since the incidence of the condition is low.

QUESTION 10

Practice annual report

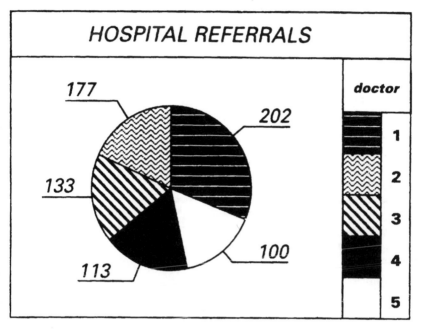

(i) Comment on the above data.
(ii) What are the possible causes of variation in hospital referrals made by each doctor?

SPECIMEN ANSWER SCHEDULE 10

1
- The candidate is expected to demonstrate the ability to extract information from a pie chart
- Doctor 1 has 202 hospital referrals, over twice that of doctor 5 (100) and also significantly more than those of any other doctor in the practice. Doctor 2 is the next highest referrer with 177
- Appreciation of limitation of gross figures, without further information e.g. list size, part/full time partners etc.
- Uncertainty of what it relates to e.g. is it in-patient, which specialty and to which hospitals?

2
- Appreciation of wide variety of hospital referrals between individual doctors and that many factors are involved
- Appreciation of difficulties when no further breakdown of information e.g. whether referred to in-patients or out-patients and which individual specialties. Also whether includes patient self referrals e.g. to casualty departments
- Appreciation of various factors involved:

a) **Patients** — the doctor may look after a particular group of patients with problems requiring referral e.g. elderly in nursing homes.

b) **GP** — special interest e.g. increased referrals for certain specialist investigation. Poorer confidence when dealing with problems in a general practice setting. Different personal list sizes, including whether trainer and trainee referrals added to responsible partner's figures. Availability e.g. part-time partners or holidays and sick/maternity leave during the study period.

APPROACH TO CURRENT AWARENESS TYPE QUESTIONS

Current awareness questions examine the candidate's knowledge of the literature in relation to current practice. Two questions are included in Paper 1. The following are examples of typical questions that have appeared in the examination:

- Summarise current thinking on antidepressant medication
- Evaluate the place of self-monitoring in asthma
- What is the evidence for the value of counsellors in general practice?

How questions are chosen

Questions will have been chosen because they are about issues that are important and very relevant to general practice. It is very likely that there will be recently published scientific evidence relating to the topic on which clinical and practice management can be based. Candidates should remember, however, that many older studies also have considerable influence.

A list of topics that have appeared in recent examinations is shown in Table 1. These are from the old Critical Reading Question (CRQ) Paper in which five such questions used to appear. The reduction in the number of questions is due to the fact that current awareness is also now being tested in Paper 2, which is machine-marked and uses a multiple choice-type format.

A candidate examining this list will recognise that it contains topics that are always going to be relevant such as diabetes, hypertension and alcohol abuse. Mixed with these are subjects which are more topical and about which there have been many recent papers. There may have been advances in treatment, such as in heart failure or the use of lipid-lowering drugs, or there may have been controversy, such as in screening for prostate cancer or prescribing third generation combined oral contraceptives. It should not therefore be too difficult for candidates to identify likely questions. Potential questions are tested on a large number of examiners before being adopted, so it is unlikely that obscure topics will pass through.

Table 1: Topics appearing in the Reading and Current Practice Section of the CRQ Paper in 1996 and 1997

May 1996	May 1997
Chronic heart failure	Evidence based medicine
Acute low back pain	Home confinement
Shared care in diabetes	Combined oral contraceptives
Mammography	Management of common viral infections
Opiate addiction	Care after a myocardial infarction
October 1996	**October 1997**
Screening for prostate cancer	Prevention of osteoporosis
Child health surveillance (The Hall report)	Health needs of teenagers
	Quality care of patients with epilepsy
Hypertension	Community mental health care
Parkinson's disease	Lipid-lowering drugs
Alcohol abuse	

How to answer questions

Candidates often express concern about answering current awareness questions. This concern centres on uncertainty about how to display knowledge of the medical literature and in particular on the need to quote references. When examiners design a question they also produce a model answer based on published literature. A candidate who is able to identify the main points in the answer will obtain a good mark. The use of relevant references will move the mark higher, particularly if some appraisal of these takes place. The following example outlines a question and its model answer.

Question

Discuss the quality of care of patients with epilepsy in general practice. What strategies have been suggested for improvement?

Answer

- Epilepsy is a common chronic illness (point prevalence 0.4—1.0%). Up to 90% are not under hospital supervision yet epilepsy has been left out of the chronic disease management payments

- Problems that have been identified with quality of care include inaccurate diagnoses, lack of systematic follow up, under treatment, polypharmacy, poor compliance, failure in GP—patient communication and a low level of recording detail in notes

- The following barriers have been identified:
  - The organisation of care including a lack of disease registers in practices and lack of support from hospitals where patients are often seen by non-neurologists
  - The general practitioner who often lacks knowledge and motivation and may worry about time and the cost of care
  - The patient who may have a low motivation to seek help often due to the stigma of epilepsy. He may also have poor knowledge about his condition which may be further complicated by co-existing mental or physical illness

- Two major nationwide initiatives have been established to improve care:
  - The epilepsy task force, a multidisciplinary group, which evolved from the panel of experts who produced the 'epilepsy needs document'. Its broad aims include a public awareness campaign, improved primary and secondary care provision, research and audit to improve services in primary care and the introduction of guidelines for management (Brown et al 1993; see page 81)
  - A liaison nurse programme between a hospital specialist epilepsy clinic and general practice. (Wellcome Foundation 1993; see page 82)

All of the material used in this answer was contained in a review article in the *British Journal of General Practice* just over 12 months before the exam (Thapar 1996; see page 82). Several other articles were also published in that period and some marks would be obtained by reference to them. However most of the marks for this sort of question would be obtained by identifying the points outlined in the model answer. Remembering where you had read about them would be less important. The information above cannot be found in textbooks so it could only have been acquired by reading recent papers.

The outline represents a perfect answer. In the short time available in the examination it is unlikely that anyone could reproduce it. It may be helpful therefore to look at what standard of answer would give a high score in terms of marks, an average score and a low score.

Range of answers and their marks

High mark: Candidates would demonstrate a wide knowledge touching at least in brief on most aspects of the model answer. It would be very clear that they had read Thapar's review article and they would probably quote other references as well.

Average mark: About half the points would be identified either evenly spread through most areas of the answer or covering one or two areas in depth (usually problems identified and barriers to care) and missing others. The use of references would usually be superficial.

Low mark: One or two areas would be touched upon but only superficially and probably by chance. Many candidates would write about the clinical management of epilepsy (investigations, drugs, monitoring etc.) Any references would be irrelevant.

In some questions being able to quote references is more important. These references will usually relate to large much publicised trials, review articles or campaigns. The example below is such a question. It also shows a variation from the traditional style of question. Here clinical scenarios are presented.

Question

Discuss any published evidence which might influence you to attempt blood pressure after serial measurement is shown.

1   A man of 58 years. He has recently suffered a transient ischaemic attack. Blood pressure 150/95.
2   A man of 40 years. His 45-year-old brother has angina. His father died of a myocardial infarction aged 50 years. Blood pressure 145/92.
3   A woman of 70 years with no cardiovascular risk factors or adverse clinical findings. Blood pressure 175/95.

Answer

In all three cases there are grounds for recommending treatment because:

- There is approximately a 40% reduction in stroke and a 15% reduction in coronary heart disease (Collins et al 1990; see page 82).
- The benefits are also seen in elderly people (Amery et al 1985, SHEP Cooperative research group 1991, Medical Research Council Working Party 1992; see pages 81-82).
- The British Hypertension Society would recommend treatment.

Further marks could be obtained in this question by pointing out that trials have used mainly diuretics and β-blockers, and that the evidence for the value of newer drugs is at present insufficient. Also, candidates would be expected to discuss the value of non-pharmacological methods of treatment and consider the importance of other risk factors.

The question looks for evidence in favour of treating mild hypertension. The scenarios involve a person with target organ damage, a person with a strong cardiovascular risk factor and an elderly person. The seminal publication on this subject is: *Management guidelines in essential hypertension;* report of the second working party of the British Hypertension Society (Sever et al 1993) and all candidates would be expected to show evidence of having read this.

The overview of drug trials by Collins et al in the *Lancet* might not have been read by candidates in its original form but many might be able to refer to some of the trials discussed in it.

It may be that you will find a question for which it will be difficult to find references from your recent reading of the journals that are relevant to the questions being asked. It is important to resist quoting articles that are related but not directly relevant. Rather, write an answer stating what you know about the subject being questioned. An example of a question which might cause this sort of difficulty is shown on page 79.

Question

Discuss the benefits of hormone replacement therapy for the prevention of
a) arterial disease, b) osteoporosis.

Answer

Arterial disease:
- Most studies used conjugated equine oestrogen without progesterone
- Oestrogen reduces LDL cholesterol and probably raises HDL cholesterol
- Ischaemic heart disease is reduced by 20% and stroke by 15%
- Benefit is seen whenever started but is lost within 2 years of stopping
- The oral route is probably more beneficial because of the 'first-pass' effect on hepatic metabolism
- Progesterone partially antagonises the beneficial effect of oestrogen.

Osteoporosis:
- Oestrogen decreases the rate of absorption of trabecula bone principally by inhibition of osteoclastic activity
- Numerous prospective placebo controlled studies show that oestrogens reduce the long term risk of fracture of the hips, wrist and spine. The reduction is generally between 50 and 60%
- To maximise skeletal benefits treatment should be started at the time of the menopause because this is the time of accelerated bone loss
- Bone loss may be arrested at any age but lost bone will not be restored
- To gain maximum benefit HRT should be taken for at least 5 years and longer if there has been a premature menopause
- Bone loss resumes on stopping oestrogen
- Progesterone does not cancel the effects of oestrogen.

There is of course a vast amount of literature on the subject of HRT but it is unlikely that candidates will have read any of the original papers, particularly as many are to be found in obscure journals in the United States. There is however a book which may be present in many practice libraries entitled *Hormone replacement therapy — your questions answered* (Whitehead and Godfree). This book answers all the questions a doctor might have about HRT, supporting the answers with the evidence. Again, showing evidence that you had read this book would improve your mark. Other acceptable reading that a candidate could refer to here would include overviews on HRT in the *Prescriber's Journal* or the *Drug and Therapeutic Bulletin*. It is however identifying what is known about the subject and backed by evidence, rather than sources of that evidence, which will attract most of the marks in this question.

A high scoring candidate would identify nine or more of these points and a poor scoring candidate less than four. Evidence of reading and the insertion of more detail would also influence the final mark.

For many of these current awareness questions there may well be other important issues that are not the sort of issues which could be supported by evidence. So, for instance, in the care of a patient after a myocardial infarction, the general practitioner is important for providing continuity of care for both the patient and the family, for his skills as a communicator and for his insight into the social and psychological processes that might affect the outcome. These and other similar attributes of a general practitioner and his interaction with patients are examined elsewhere in the written papers. It is important to distinguish questions requiring evidence from those which do not in order to avoid wasted effort, for in a current awareness question discussion of such issues will not attract marks. Examination development may well result in more integration of questions and candidates will need to remain alert for possible subtle changes. The advice to 'read the question carefully' holds good even at this level.

With just over 15 minutes to answer a question it is not advisable to attempt to produce essay answers. By using an expanded note form a lot of information can be put down on paper. Also this makes it easier for examiners to mark. However if abbreviations are used it is important to make sure that they are used commonly enough for the examiner to know what they mean.

How to prepare for the examination

Critical reading should be a lifelong activity which is a part of our continuing professional development. However, those who feel the need to make some special preparation for the examination should concentrate on the *British Medical Journal* and the *British Journal of General Practice.* Certainly the preceding 2 years' issues should be worked through. The title of every article should be read and, where it has relevance for general practice, candidates should at least read the summary. Interest or the fact that the article is contributing to the body of knowledge on a 'hot topic' should inspire candidates to read further.

The topics in Table 1 (page 74) could form a starting point for anyone assembling a list of 'hot topics'. It is worth gathering together papers under topic headings and keeping them in a file. Many trainers may already have done this, so all that is required is to add recent information and identify any new topics which seem important. Particularly important are editorials, review articles and many of the *Occasional Papers of the Royal College of General Practitioners.* These are useful for building up a wider picture of published work. In order to build up the full picture of a particular subject it may be necessary to do a library search or use Medline or the Internet. Groups of candidates meeting together to share out information gathering and to discuss topics saves time and is a very useful exercise.

Candidates often worry about current awareness questions more than they do about other parts of the examination. They are only about keeping up to date, something which all of us should surely do. If there is a topic about which you think you know little, remember that it only forms a small proportion of the overall examination in terms of marks so there is no need to panic. Write down what you know. You are bound to score some marks.

References

Amery A, Birkenhager W, Brixo P, et al (1985) Mortality and morbidity results from the European Working Party in the Elderly Trial. *Lancet* , 1, 1349—1354.

Brown S, Bretts T, Chadwick D, et al (1993) An epilepsy needs document. *Seizure* , 2, 91—103.

Collins R, Peto R, MacMahon S, et al (1990) Blood pressure, stroke and coronary heart disease. Part 2. Short-term reductions in blood pressure: overview of randomised drug trials in their epidemiological context. *Lancet* , 335, 827—38.

Medical Research Council Working Party (1992) MRC trial of treatment of hypertension in older adults, principal results. *British Medical Journal*, 304, 405—12.

Sever P, Beevers G, Bulpitt C, et al (1993) Management guidelines in essential hypertension: Report of the second working party of the British Hypertension Society. *British Medical Journal*, 306, 983—7.

SHEP Co-operative Research Group (1991) Prevention of stroke by anti-hypertensive drug treatment in older persons with isolated systolic hypertension. *Journal of the American Medical Association*, 265, 3255—64.

Thapar AK (1996) Care of patients with epilepsy in the community: will new initiatives address old problems? *British Journal of General Practice*, 46, 37—42.

Wellcome Foundation (1993) Epilepsy liaison nurse programme: a management protocol for epilepsy in general practice. Crewe, Wellcome Foundation.

Whitehead M, Godfree V, (1992) Hormone replacement therapy — your questions answered. Churchill Livingstone.

APPROACH TO MODIFIED ESSAY QUESTION (PROBLEM SOLVING) TYPE QUESTIONS

The old style MEQ Paper has a long and distinguished history, testing candidates' decision making and their ability to translate theoretical knowledge into practice, highlighting their attitudes and values, their ability to deal with complex and unexpected situations and their understanding of the doctor's role in all its contexts. The new style Paper 1 will have six questions based on the old MEQ type format, which tests candidates' ability to integrate and apply theoretical knowledge and professional values to practical problems encountered in an NHS setting. These are known as Problem Solving Questions. The marking of these questions is time-consuming and currently computer methods of marking are being investigated. These questions may therefore be found in Paper 2.

The area covered

The candidate is expected to appreciate the whole range of problems that the average general practitioner could expect to come across in practice — clinical, ethical, administrative or concerning self-awareness and development.

What the examiners are looking for

Questions may present a problem which you have never experienced before, but the examiners are looking for the principles of problem solving which are no different to those used every day, and expect the candidate to understand the key issues that are presented. These key issues are known as **'constructs'**. A construct is a theme, a strand, a dimension, one of a number of 'nubs' the question may have.

Each candidate is provided with a combined question and answer booklet, and each page goes to a different examiner so it is important not to refer to things that have been written in answer to a previous question. The examiners mark the paper by reference to how the candidate performs in the main constructs. The examiners have a marking schedule that considers about five constructs per question, and these constructs are chosen to be as separate from each other as possible, so that a candidate may do well in one independently of performance in another. Overlapping themes would unfairly penalise a candidate twice if the concept was missed.

Examples of constructs

- Clinical competence
- Consultation skills
- Awareness of patient's hidden agenda
- Recognition of patient's point of view
- Ability to predict future developments
- Cost effectiveness
- Follow-up arrangements
- Insight into family/social influences on outcome
- Preventive interventions
- Financial and business acumen
- Awareness of ethical considerations
- Involvement of other team members
- Awareness of doctor's own feelings/motivation
- Clinical safety
- 'Caritas' — sense of genuine caring or empathy
- Logical and systematic approach.

The candidate's performance relating to each construct is graded from 0 to 5:

0 **Non existent**. No mention is made at all of the particular construct and it appears the candidate did not seem to consider it.

1 **Bad**. The candidate appears to acknowledge the construct's existence by implication or in passing but does not develop it to any degree. Its meaning may have been misunderstood, its significance not perceived or responses to it may be inappropriate.

2 **Mediocre**. The construct is explicitly mentioned but there is little evidence that it is really understood. Discussion may be sketchy or jargon ridden. Examples may be too few or too non-specific to display an acceptable level of understanding.

3 **Satisfactory**. The candidate satisfies the examiner that the essentials of the construct are adequately understood, though without particular flair.

4 **Good**. The candidate clearly demonstrates a better grasp of the construct than most. There is good detail and description, though a few relatively minor points may be omitted.

5 **Excellent**. The candidate shows a superior coverage of the construct both in principle and in detail.

The actual constructs that the examiners use in the marking brief describe what a good candidate would be expected to do on a good day, recognising the time constraints of the surgery. It is thus important to think widely since if one construct is missed it is only possible to obtain 80% of the marks. To gain a high mark it is important to be aware of the breadth **and** the depth of each construct. The final mark will take the form of a pass, fail or merit for the best 25% or so of candidates.

How to maximise your marks and how to approach the question

- Think yourself into the situation. Many of the questions are based on real experiences that the examiners have been through. What are the problems in the described situation? Do not forget the feelings that you may have when faced with the situation (self-awareness). It is important to think widely and divergently, and also to think how you would approach the situation on an ideal day if you had adequate time and resources.

- Think of the key themes that this question is beginning to highlight — these are the constructs.

- Write short notes on each of the constructs, expanding as much as possible so that the examiner can appreciate how much (or how little!) you know about this area. It is important to remember that the examiner is looking to see whether you actually understand what the construct is about rather than just regurgitating bland terms e.g. ideas, concerns and expectations. Many people ask: How much should I write? The secret is to try to get as much information down as you can in the allotted time per question, which is 15 minutes.

- Remember — keep a close eye on the time. Answering the questions within the time constraints is an important skill. Legible and concise note form is the preferred method.

- Don't panic!

Example

Your Practice Manager has received a letter of complaint from a patient who has recently had a cervical smear performed by one of your male partners. The patient states that she found the procedure very embarrassing and that she felt that a chaperone should have been present. Discuss the implications of this letter.

A good candidate will be expected to cover the following constructs:

Medico legal
Appreciation of the need for a chaperone, respect for patient's privacy and confidentiality.

Practice organisation
Review and establishment of practice policy, method of dealing with complaints.

Problem solving
Method of reply, considering the consequences of each proposed intervention.

Self-awareness
Annoyance at patient or partner. Understanding own vulnerability and concern for the future.

Duties to a colleague
Empathy and support for colleague. Colleague experiencing difficulties.

Write your answers in the space provided. Your answers should be brief and may take the form of lists rather than lengthy descriptions. The answers are given after each question.

Question 1

Gemma Smith, aged 15 years, attends accompanied by her mother. She complains of a vaginal discharge. Her mother stays in the consulting room while you examine Gemma with the practice nurse as chaperone in a separate room. She tells you that she had sexual intercourse a week ago but asks you not to tell her mother.

Outline your management.

Answer 1

The good candidate would be expected to consider the following:

Ethics	Gemma's autonomy and right to confidentiality, recognise that she is a minor, duty to Gemma and also to her mother.
Communication	Talking to Gemma (eliciting her concerns and teenager communication difficulties), what to tell her mother, encourage her to discuss the situation with mother and family.
Clinical management	Vaginal discharge, contraception,? STD, consider possibility of pregnancy,? refer.
Prevention	Contraception, reducing risks STD/HIV, other life style advice.
Practice organisation	Follow-up, consider health care needs of teenagers and making surgery teenager-friendly.

Question 2

Brian Oatley is a 58-year-old carpenter and a heavy smoker. He has come for the result of a recent day-case bronchoscopy, which revealed a bronchial carcinoma. He has not been told of the findings.

How would you handle this situation?

Answer 2

A good candidate would be expected to consider the following:

Communication	Establish rapport/empathy, check patient's understanding, plan hierarchy of giving information and check understanding at each stage, deal with denial/strong emotions.
Practice organisation	Make time for doctor and patient, consider presence of spouse/friend/nurse.
Ethics	Patient autonomy — right to know the diagnosis but balance with right not to know information if patient does not wish. Offer patient the opportunity to say first whether he wants all the information.
Patient centredness	Negotiation of management plan.
Clinical management	Immediate management of haemoptysis/other symptoms. Long-term – referral options.
Self-awareness	Feelings towards patient, feelings towards hospital. Coping with possible strong patient's reaction, readiness to see next patient.

Question 3

You are on call for your practice and at 11pm you are telephoned by Tracey Tyler. Her 5-month-old son, Billy, has been passing bright red blood in his stools for the past 24 hours. She says he is well in himself.

What issues does this consultation raise?

Answer 3

A good candidate would be expected to consider the following:

Clinical management   Assess medical needs, consider visit, advice over telephone.

Practice organisation   Logistics of night visit, use of out of hours services, night visit fee.

Communication   Establish mother's concerns and health beliefs, clear information gathering and advice over telephone.

Altering help-seeking behaviour   Consider principles.

Self-awareness   Anger at time, minor complaints.

Question 4

You are called out of surgery by Barry Tallman, who is a 67-year-old retired chef. He has a 4 hour history of central chest pain. He looks well and on examination he has a BP of 130/80 and a regular pulse of 98 beats per minute. You diagnose that he has a probable myocardial infarction.

How do you decide to manage him?

Approach to Modified Essay Question (Problem Solving) Type Questions

Answer 4

A good candidate would be expected to consider the following:

Clinical management	Establish diagnosis, consider use of thrombolysis, give immediate dose of aspirin, consider use of ECG, referral strategies.
Evidence based approach	Knowledge of studies of home versus hospital care, knowledge of use of aspirin and thrombolysis.
Patient centredness	Patient choice/preference, patient's concerns and health beliefs.
Psycho-social awareness	Aware of psycho-social factors e.g. living alone, adverse social circumstances.
Self-awareness	Confidence/competence in dealing with the problem, ease of follow-up.

Question 5

Carol Hanson, a 42-year-old part-time secretary, enters your surgery and bursts into tears. She states that she has just discovered that her accountant husband has been having an affair with a junior colleague.

What would you hope to achieve by the end of this consultation?

Answer 5

A good candidate would be expected to consider the following:

Communication	Establish rapport, negotiation of options, focus on the patient's ideas and concerns.
Clinical management	Exclude depression, arrangements for follow-up.
Psycho-social support	Self and friends, voluntary and statutory.
'Caritas'	Empathy and caring.
Practice organisation	Time constraints during a busy surgery, arrangements for follow-up.

Question 6

Jim Connoll is a 44-year-old electrician and presents with a 10 day history of low back pain, which is not settling despite rest. He would like you to refer him to an osteopath.

How would you respond?

Answer 6

A good candidate would be expected to consider the following:

Communication	Establish patient's ideas, concerns and health beliefs about low back pain and osteopathy, hidden agenda?
Ethics	Respect patient's autonomy about choice of alternative practitioner.
Clinical management	Management of low back pain, exclusion of serious illness, role of clinical examination.
Evidence based approach	Guidelines on low back pain, research on benefits of osteopath versus physiotherapy.
Self-awareness	Personal views and tolerance on role of complementary medicine.

Question 7

You are called into reception by your receptionist. Darren, a known drug addict, is shouting and demanding to be seen immediately.

How do you manage this situation?

Answer 7

A good candidate would be expected to consider the following:

Communication	Dealing with angry patient.
Practice organisation	Emergency appointments, balance of priorities with other patients, reception staff training.
Teamwork	Important to have unified response, especially after traumatic event.
Clinical management	Management of presenting complaint, including drug addiction.
Self-awareness	Annoyance at patient, and how it affects management of current patients and following patients.

Question 8

At the end of surgery you are visited by a pharmaceutical company representative who asks if you would like to attend an all expenses paid scientific meeting in Rome. The subject area is one which interests you.

What issues does this invitation raise?

Answer 8

A good candidate would be expected to consider the following:

Ethical   GMC rules on acceptance of hospitality, feeling of obligation to the representative in the future, alteration in prescribing pattern, relationship with representative in the future.

Professional education/ self development   Assessment of educational event, assessment of own learning needs.

Practice organisation Time, locum cover, incidental expenses.

Problem solving   Consider cost versus benefits in attending meeting.

Self-awareness   Balancing ethical considerations against cheap method of obtaining PGEA, effect of decision on relationship with representative in the future, relationship with other colleagues in practice.

Question 9

Following a practice meeting brainstorming session, you produce a list of proposed practice audits.

How do you decide which one to proceed with?

Answer 9

A good candidate would be expected to consider the following:

Practice organisation	Resource implications, costs versus benefits to the practice, organisational difficulties.
Problem solving	Prioritise, relevance, feasibility, cost versus benefit considerations.
Personal and professional growth	Addressing learning needs, personal commitment or enjoyment of the subject.
Teamwork	Involving other members of the primary health care team and developing working relationships.
Wider NHS context	Response to local health needs, Health of the Nation targets, requirement for chronic disease management payments.

Question 10

Your Practice Manager informs you of the need to purchase a new autoclave, costing £2,000, since the old one is beyond repair.

What factors would you expect to take into account in the decision to replace it?

Answer 10

A good candidate would be expected to consider the following:

Problem solving	Requirement of autoclave in the future, possible further uses of autoclave, work load considerations.
Practice organisation	Delegation for maintenance, training in use.
Financial and business	Planning method of purchase/lease/hire, service contract.
Teamwork	Involve all concerned, respecting autonomy of main users e.g. practice nurse decision.
Self-awareness	Reluctance to spend large sums of money, conflicting priorities, feeling of anger or blame.

Question 11

Your attached district nurse would like to introduce an evidence and research based approach to the management of leg ulcers in your patients.

Discuss the implications of this approach.

Answer 11

A good candidate would be expected to consider the following:

Respect for fellow professionals	Consider autonomy, training and responsibilities.
Practice organisation	Protocol and referral pathways development, audit possible?
Communication	Need to have common understanding of what is meant by evidence and research based approach, hidden agenda of district nurse?
Teamwork	Opportunity to work together jointly, other community staff involved or only practice nurse?
Self-awareness	Lack of knowledge of the proposed approach, feelings about change and delegation of duties to nursing colleagues.

Question 12

Pat, your practice nurse, is due to retire in 4 months time. The partnership decides to draw up a new job description.

How would you decide what to include in the job description?

Answer 12

A good candidate would be expected to consider the following:

Practice organisation	Hours, pay and conditions, who reports to, qualifications required.
Problem solving	Logical approach considering present needs, future needs, skills mix required.
Team working	Practice dynamics and type of personality required to work in existing primary health care team.
Primary care development	Extended role of the practice nurse and nurse practitioners.
Role of professional colleague	Delegation versus autonomy, health professional in their own right.

APPROACH TO MULTIPLE CHOICE AND COMPUTER MARKED QUESTIONS

MCQ type questions form the basis for Paper 2 which is designed to test the extent of a candidate's knowledge about general practice, including both established and recent knowledge.

Questions in Paper 2 are developed by a group of examiners and are derived from reference sources, including review articles and original papers in journals readily available to all general practitioners — this includes the *British Medical Journal, The British Journal of General Practice, Evidence Based Medicine* and the *Drug and Therapeutics Bulletin*.

Paper 2 will be a composite paper which will comprise the traditional MCQ paper and components of the Critical Reading Paper. What will emerge will be 'a new look' paper called 'The Machine Markable Paper.' This will last for three hours and will cover the areas of factual knowledge, current literature, critical appraisal, statistics, epidemiology and research design and 'best practice' using evidence based medicine.

You should expect questions on a broad range of relevant general practice topics

- Critical appraisal — including knowledge of statistics and research methodology sufficient to evaluate published papers
- General medicine and surgery
- Medical specialties (e.g. dermatology, ophthalmology and ENT)
- Women's health
- Child health
- Service management.

Machine markable paper structure

The paper will contain a similar number of questions to the old MCQ paper and will consist of standard true/false items, extended matching items, single best answers, tables or written material to appraise either in true/false format or by selecting the most appropriate word from a menu of choices reflecting the most accurate critique.

Section 1

This contains questions of the multiple choice true/false variety. There is a statement, or stem, followed by various items, any or all of which may be true or false. The number of items per question may vary up to a maximum of six. There are a maximum of 400 true/false items in the examination paper but there may be fewer.

Example MCQ

The signs and symptoms of Parkinsonism	
1 characteristically remain unilateral for years	T
2 are a recognised side-effect of amitriptyline therapy	F
3 are a recognised sequel to encephalitis	T
4 characteristically include intention tremor	F

Section 2

This contains, firstly, questions of the extended matching variety. These typically consist of a scenario which has to be matched to an answer from a list of options. For any one item the candidate must choose one, and only one, of the options. Usually there will be more options than items. Secondly, there may also be questions of the single best answer variety. These consist of a statement or stem followed by a variable number of items, only one of which is correct. There will be a maximum of 100 items in the second section but there may be fewer.

Example extended matching question

Options:

A   Basilar migraine
B   Cerebral tumour
C   Cranial arteritis
D   Macular degeneration
E   Occlusion of the central retinal artery
F   Occlusion of the central retinal vein
G   Optic neuritis (demyelinating)
H   Retinal detachment
I   Tobacco optic neuropathy

Instruction:

For each patient with reduced vision, select the single most likely diagnosis. Each option can be used once, more than once, or not at all.

Items:

1   A 75-year-old man, who is a heavy smoker, with blood pressure of 170/105, complains of floaters in the right eye for many months and flashing lights in bright sunlight. He has now noticed a 'curtain' across vision in the right eye.   **H**

2   A 70-year-old woman complains of shadows which sometimes obscure her vision for a few minutes. She has felt unwell recently with loss of weight and face pain when chewing food.   **C**

3   A 45-year-old woman, who is a heavy smoker, with blood pressure of 170/110, complains of impaired vision in the left eye. She has difficulty discriminating colours and has noticed that her eye aches when looking to the side.   **G**

Areas to be Examined

a)   Current literature

Keeping up to date is a very important aspect of personal and professional development. It is therefore essential that this is tested in the MRCGP examination. The questions refer to articles that have been published in the preceding 12 to 18 months. Guidance to candidates is that current literature will be about articles that the 'average' general practitioner would be expected to read. This means that questions will be drawn from the *British Medical Journal, British Journal of Medical Practice* and *Drug and Therapeutics Bulletin*. Questions may also be asked about major trials that have had an impact on day-to-day patient management, for example ISIS2 and the European Working Party on Hypertension in the Elderly.

Candidates will not be expected to be able to remember details of the actual study design but the key messages from papers, and the evidence on which everyday clinical decisions are based will be tested.

The criteria for choosing the material are that it:

- should be relevant to current general practice
- should test the range of the candidate's ability
- should be a common topic (recognised by the majority of general practitioners)
- should be an important topic (likely to change or impact on general practice)
- requires critical appraisal skills
- should favour the well-read doctor.

Examples of standard true/false items

Current evidence concerning the effectiveness of routine mammography suggests that in the UK

1   the screening age be lowered to 40 years   F
2   two-view mammography at each screening is cost effective   T
3   the screening interval be reduced to 2 years   T
4   mammograms should be read by two independent
    radiologists   T
5   mammography has been shown to be successful in reducing
    the mortality from breast cancer   F

The goals for the St Vincent Joint Task Force on Diabetes include reduction in

1   micro albuminuria   F
2   retinopathic damage   T
3   prevalence of hypertension   F
4   the number of limb amputations   T
5   morbidity and mortality from coronary heart
    disease   T

Backache in pregnancy, (*BMJ* April 1997)

1   affects 50% of pregnant women at some stage of pregnancy T
2   is less prevalent than backache in non-pregnant women   F
3   is associated with older women   F
4   is more likely with unrewarding employment   T
5   is reported more frequently in prospective studies   T

Examples of extended matching items

Match the most appropriate statement from these seminal papers on treatment of hypertension in the elderly.

1	**EWPHE**
2	**STOP trial**
3	**SHEP**
4	**MRC trial**

A	Showed benefit from treating isolated systolic BP >160	3
B	Hydrochlorothiazide and amiloride reduced the risk of stroke, coronary events and all CV events in older hypertensives	4
C	The phenomenon of increased mortality with low BP in patients treated with hypertension was shown to be not due to treatment but rather associated with other causes of ill health	1
D	Described non-drug approaches	
E	Showed drop in total mortality in patients 70 — 84 with elevated systolic and diastolic BP	2

Topic: The prevention, aetiology and treatment of ischaemic heart disease

Options
a   J shaped curve
b   Cost effective after 5 years
c   Reduces risk of sudden death
d   Management of hypercholesterolaemia
e   Effectiveness of Enalapril
f   Higher risk of coronary disease
g   Lowers HDL cholesterol
h   Management of stable angina
i   Cardioprotective

Match each of the items below with an option a — i from above. Items from the option list may appear once, more than once or not at all.

1	North of England evidence based guidelines development project (*BMJ* 1996)	h
2	Moderate alcohol consumption	i
3	Low flavanoid intake	f
4	Elderly hypertensive men with diastolic bood pressure < 90	a
5	Elevated C reactive protein	f
6	Ox-check study	b

b)   Critical appraisal

Critical appraisal is an essential skill for all practising doctors and can probably be defined as the application of common sense, a questioning attitude and analytical thought in assessing the quality of information obtained from written material. This material would include such things as research papers but also letters from hospital consultants or even something as straightforward as an audit or laboratory report. The formats of these questions may be in the traditional true/false format but there will be an increasing number of extended matching items or a short critique where the candidate has to 'fill in the blanks' by choosing from a menu of options.

Examples of various true/false matching items, and selection of the most appropriate word from a menu of choices reflecting the most accurate critique

Retirement on grounds of ill health in six organisations (A, B, C, D, E and F)

Detail	A	B	C	D	E	F
Normal retirement age (years)	65	55	55	60	60	65
Ill health retirement per 10,000 contributing members	20	250	177	111	110	180
Mode age (years)	62	46	48	54	56	56
Mode length of service (years)	14	27	27	32	5	18

The results above would suggest that

a   financial enhancement packages may have been offered in organisations B and C   T
b   stricter medical criteria are used in organisation F than in other organisations   F
c   occupation A has the lowest morbidity   T

Geometric mean scores on Edinburgh Postnatal Depression Scale for patients who completed the study

Assessment time

Treatment (drug plus sessions of counselling)	Number of patients	Baseline	1 week	12 weeks
Fluoxetine:				
Plus 1 session	16	16.4	12.8	5.4
Plus 6 sessions	13	16.9	10.9	5.3
Placebo:				
Plus 1 session	17	17.4	14.2	9.8
Plus 6 sessions	15	16.8	14.2	9.9
Total fluoxetine	29	16.6	11.9	5.3
Total placebo	32	17.1	14.2	8.9
Total 1 session counselling	33	16.9	13.5	7.4
Total 6 sessions counselling	28	16.9	12.6	6.6

Scores over 9 and over 12 can be used as screening thresholds

The results suggest that

a fluoxetine and counselling were effective in treating postnatal depression T
b fluoxetine was more effective than counselling alone F
c a single session of counselling was as effective as six sessions of counselling F
d differences at 12 weeks in those having one session of counselling and six sessions was statistically significant F
e fluoxetine was superior to placebo in outcome measures T
f the response to fluoxetine was evident within 1 week T

c) Statistics, epidemiology and research design

The format of these questions will again be true/false style or extended matching items. Candidates are not expected to be expert statisticians as the examiners setting the papers certainly are not!

Examples of extended matching questions and the true/false style

---

Results of colorectal cancer screening using rectal examination and faecal occult bloods

Colorectal cancer

	Disease present	Disease absent
Screening + ve	120	60
Screening - ve	80	740

a	has a sensitivity of 72%	F
b	has a specificity of 92.5%	T
c	has a predictive value of 60%	F
d	has comparatively high sensitivity	F
e	the probability that a person with a negative test does not have the disease is approximately 10%	T

Electrocardiographic findings	Impaired left ventricular systolic function	Preserved left ventricular systolic function	Total
Abnormal	90	169	259
Normal	6	269	275
Total	96	438	534

Options:

A	$\frac{90}{438}$	E	$\frac{169}{259}$	I	$\frac{269}{275}$
B	$\frac{90}{275}$	F	$\frac{90}{259}$	J	$\frac{96}{438}$
C	$\frac{90}{96}$	G	$\frac{269}{534}$	K	$\frac{96}{534}$
D	$\frac{169}{438}$	H	$\frac{269}{438}$	L	$\frac{169}{534}$

Match item 1 – 4 below with the correct option A – L. Each option can only be used once.

1	Sensitivity	C
2	Specificity	H
3	Positive predictive value	F
4	Negative predictive value	I

For each of the following research studies select the study type that most closely describes it.

A   Case controlled study
B   Randomised double blind cross-over trial
C   Cohort study
D   Randomised double blind placebo-controlled trial
E   Descriptive study

1   A population of children living close to a nuclear power station was matched with another population of children living close to a conventional power station. They were each followed over a number of years to see if there was an excess incidence of leukaemia in either group.   **C**

2   A researcher into the causes of SIDS (sudden infant death syndrome) matched each of a group of children who were the victims of SIDS with a healthy child of the same age, sex and social class. He then established the usual sleeping position of each child to test the hypothesis that sleeping prone was a causative factor in the disease.   **A**

3   A psychiatrist wondered if psychopathic personality disorders might be the result of maternal drug abuse during pregnancy. He therefore investigated the background of a number of psychopaths to see if their mothers had ever abused drugs while they were pregnant.   **E**

4   To test whether Drug A was better than Drug B in the treatment of rheumatoid arthritis, patients were allocated randomly to one or the other. After a period of time they were assessed to establish changes in pain, stiffness and joint swelling. They were then changed onto the other drug, and the assessment repeated after the same period of time. Until the end of the study neither the researcher nor patients knew which drug was which.   **B**

5   To see if a new topical preparation for psoriasis is effective, patients were randomly allocated to either the preparation or its base without the active drug. After a period of time they were assessed to establish the degree of improvement (if any). Until the end of the study neither patients nor researchers knew which treatment had been used.   **D**

For each study, select the most appropriate study design from the following letter options. Each option can be used once, more than once, or not all.

A   Correlation study
B   Case-control study
C   Cohort study
D   Clinical trial
E   Descriptive study
F   Meta-analysis

1   A survey is conducted to determine the prevalence of mitral valve prolapse within the general population. **E**

2   The prior use of aspirin is compared among 500 patients with newly diagnosed colon cancer and 1000 healthy persons. **B**

3   Prevention of lung cancer is studied within a population of 12,000 smokers who are assigned randomly to receive either vitamin E and beta-carotene or an inert substance. **D**

4   The reported national incidence rates of hepatitis B infection are associated with corresponding national mortality rates for liver cancer. **A**

5   The results of several investigations of exposure to environmental tobacco smoke and risk of lung cancer are combined to reach a summary conclusion. **F**

Randomised controlled trials in general practice

1   are impossible to perform   F
2   are particularly prone to selection bias   T
3   may be difficult to carry out in an average sized practice T
4   are well suited to the general practice culture   F

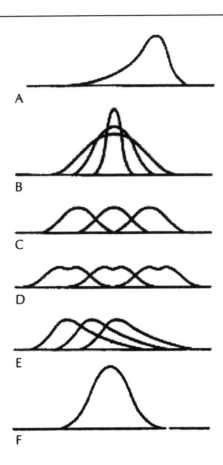

Match the lettered illustrations with the following distributions:

1	Negatively skewed	**A**
2	Equal variances with different means	**C**
3	Normal	**F**
4	Positively skewed	**E**
5	Bimodal	**D**
6	Equal means with different variances	**B**

d)   'The best practice'

The main objective in this area is to identify if candidates are using current evidence on which to base their everyday clinical decisions. The format of these questions will be 'single best answers' using clinical vignettes. Although these are very time consuming to construct they are the most reliable way of testing candidates' knowledge. The examiners will develop these questions based on the best evidence currently available. It is important to remember that several of the answers may be acceptable practice but the examiners are looking for the single best answer supported by the strongest evidence.

The single best answer questions usually consist of a description of a clinical scenario. The item vignette is followed by four or five response options lettered a, b, c, d, e. The candidate will be required to select the best answer to the question. Other options may well be partially correct but there is only ONE BEST ANSWER. The best way to answer these questions is to read the patient description of each item carefully and be certain that you understand what is being asked. You should try to generate an answer and then look for that in the option list. It is important to read each option carefully eliminating those that are clearly incorrect. Of the remaining options, you should select the one that you believe to be the most correct and mark it on the appropriate space on the answer sheet.

Examples of true/false and single best answer format

True/false format

Stroke prevention in atrial fibrillation	
Current evidence shows that	
1 warfarin is most effective when INR is 2.0	T
2 aspirin is ineffective	F
3 fixed dose warfarin and aspirin are more effective than warfarin alone	F
4 dipyridamole is effective	F
5 anticoagulation should be avoided in patients over 75 years	F

Single best answer format

Stroke prevention in atrial fibrillation

A 70-year-old man is found to have non-rheumatic atrial fibrillation, controlled on digoxin. He has had no significant previous medical problems. Choose from the list below the single best management on current evidence.

1   aspirin 150 mg daily
2   fixed dose combination of warfarin and aspirin
3   dipyridamole 200 mg bd
4   warfarin, with INR between 1.7 and 2.5
5   warfarin, with INR between 2.0 and 4.0

Answer no. 5

Reference: Stroke prevention in atrial fibrillation, Editorial *BMJ* 31 May 1997 and *BMJ* 24 May 1997.

How to approach the MCQ-type questions

It is important to be aware from the outset that the scoring of all the stems is exactly the same irrespective of the format. Candidates are awarded one mark for each item answered correctly and marks are not deducted for incorrect answers or failure to answer. This encourages candidates to attempt all items.

It is important for candidates to read the stem carefully and each of its following questions individually in order to be clear about the question asked. Certain trigger words are used in MCQ-type questions and it is important to have a clear understanding of their meaning.

Trigger words used in MCQ-type questions

- **Pathognomonic, diagnostic, characteristic** and **in the vast majority** imply that a feature will occur in at least 90% of cases
- **Typically, frequently, significantly, commonly** and **in a substantial majority** imply that a feature would occur in at least 60% of cases
- **In the majority** implies that a feature occurs in more than 50% of cases
- **In the minority** implies that a feature occurs in less than 50% of cases
- **Low chance** and **in a substantial minority** imply that a feature may occur in up to 30% of cases
- **Has been shown, recognised** and **reported** all refer to evidence which can be found in an authoritative medical text. None of these terms makes any implication about the frequency with which the feature occurs.

Candidates are required to fill in an answer sheet by shading in a lozenge. A specimen of the marking sheet is shown on page 128. It may sound obvious but it is vital to ensure that the correct lozenges are filled in since the sheets are marked by computer and if you inadvertently fill in the wrong line of answers the score could be disastrous! If you wish to change an answer your mark should be erased as fully as possible and the new answer entered. Detailed instructions will be given at the time of sitting the examination.

The Royal College of General Practitioners

SURNAME (Use block capitals)

INITIALS

INSTRUCTIONS	HOW TO MARK
✎ Use black lead pencil only (HB)	Not like these:
✎ Do NOT use ink or ballpoint pen	
✎ Make heavy black marks that fill the lozenge completely	
✎ Erase cleanly any answer you wish to change	But like this:
✎ Make no stray marks on this sheet	

ENTER CANDIDATE
NUMBER HERE ☞

NOW SHOW THE
NUMBER BY MARKING

THE GRID ☞

☞ Each of the items in the first part of the question paper is either true or false. If you believe that the answer is true, you should fill in the T lozenge; if you believe that it is false, fill in the F lozenge

☞ Enter your answers to items 1 to 150 on this side then turn over and continue entering your answers on the other side. Your question paper may contain fewer than the 400 items allowed for this sheet.

1 ⊤ ⊥   31 ⊤ ⊥   61 ⊤ ⊥   91 ⊤ ⊥   121 ⊤ ⊥
2 ⊤ ⊥   32 ⊤ ⊥   62 ⊤ ⊥   92 ⊤ ⊥   122 ⊤ ⊥
3 ⊤ ⊥   33 ⊤ ⊥   63 ⊤ ⊥   93 ⊤ ⊥   123 ⊤ ⊥
4 ⊤ ⊥   34 ⊤ ⊥   64 ⊤ ⊥   94 ⊤ ⊥   124 ⊤ ⊥
5 ⊤ ⊥   35 ⊤ ⊥   65 ⊤ ⊥   95 ⊤ ⊥   125 ⊤ ⊥
6 ⊤ ⊥   36 ⊤ ⊥   66 ⊤ ⊥   96 ⊤ ⊥   126 ⊤ ⊥
7 ⊤ ⊥   37 ⊤ ⊥   67 ⊤ ⊥   97 ⊤ ⊥   127 ⊤ ⊥
8 ⊤ ⊥   38 ⊤ ⊥   68 ⊤ ⊥   98 ⊤ ⊥   128 ⊤ ⊥
9 ⊤ ⊥   39 ⊤ ⊥   69 ⊤ ⊥   99 ⊤ ⊥   129 ⊤ ⊥
10 ⊤ ⊥   40 ⊤ ⊥   70 ⊤ ⊥   100 ⊤ ⊥   130 ⊤ ⊥
11 ⊤ ⊥   41 ⊤ ⊥   71 ⊤ ⊥   101 ⊤ ⊥   131 ⊤ ⊥
12 ⊤ ⊥   42 ⊤ ⊥   72 ⊤ ⊥   102 ⊤ ⊥   132 ⊤ ⊥
13 ⊤ ⊥   43 ⊤ ⊥   73 ⊤ ⊥   103 ⊤ ⊥   133 ⊤ ⊥
14 ⊤ ⊥   44 ⊤ ⊥   74 ⊤ ⊥   104 ⊤ ⊥   134 ⊤ ⊥
15 ⊤ ⊥   45 ⊤ ⊥   75 ⊤ ⊥   105 ⊤ ⊥   135 ⊤ ⊥
16 ⊤ ⊥   46 ⊤ ⊥   76 ⊤ ⊥   106 ⊤ ⊥   136 ⊤ ⊥
17 ⊤ ⊥   47 ⊤ ⊥   77 ⊤ ⊥   107 ⊤ ⊥   137 ⊤ ⊥
18 ⊤ ⊥   48 ⊤ ⊥   78 ⊤ ⊥   108 ⊤ ⊥   138 ⊤ ⊥
19 ⊤ ⊥   49 ⊤ ⊥   79 ⊤ ⊥   109 ⊤ ⊥   139 ⊤ ⊥
20 ⊤ ⊥   50 ⊤ ⊥   80 ⊤ ⊥   110 ⊤ ⊥   140 ⊤ ⊥
21 ⊤ ⊥   51 ⊤ ⊥   81 ⊤ ⊥   111 ⊤ ⊥   141 ⊤ ⊥
22 ⊤ ⊥   52 ⊤ ⊥   82 ⊤ ⊥   112 ⊤ ⊥   142 ⊤ ⊥
23 ⊤ ⊥   53 ⊤ ⊥   83 ⊤ ⊥   113 ⊤ ⊥   143 ⊤ ⊥
24 ⊤ ⊥   54 ⊤ ⊥   84 ⊤ ⊥   114 ⊤ ⊥   144 ⊤ ⊥
25 ⊤ ⊥   55 ⊤ ⊥   85 ⊤ ⊥   115 ⊤ ⊥   145 ⊤ ⊥
26 ⊤ ⊥   56 ⊤ ⊥   86 ⊤ ⊥   116 ⊤ ⊥   146 ⊤ ⊥
27 ⊤ ⊥   57 ⊤ ⊥   87 ⊤ ⊥   117 ⊤ ⊥   147 ⊤ ⊥
28 ⊤ ⊥   58 ⊤ ⊥   88 ⊤ ⊥   118 ⊤ ⊥   148 ⊤ ⊥
29 ⊤ ⊥   59 ⊤ ⊥   89 ⊤ ⊥   119 ⊤ ⊥   149 ⊤ ⊥
30 ⊤ ⊥   60 ⊤ ⊥   90 ⊤ ⊥   120 ⊤ ⊥   150 ⊤ ⊥

Reproduced by kind permission of the Royal College of General Practitioners

Having read the question you are faced with three possibilities:

1   You can answer the question. Good! Answer as you think best.
2   You are not sure of the answer but can use your knowledge and reasoning to work out an answer. Many of the questions will fall into this category and you may well be able to work out the correct answer.
3   You have no idea what the answer is. Because you do not lose a mark for a wrong answer — guess!

One technique is to work through the paper answering those questions that you are fairly certain about and then to go back to any questions you wish to think about again. Repeatedly going over questions you have answered can be counter productive, as answers which you were originally confident were correct may appear rather less convincing at a second, third or fourth perusal! In this situation first thoughts are usually best. Remember the examiners are not trying to trip you — they just need to find out how much you actually know! Do not try to look for hidden meanings, catches and ambiguities. Undoubtedly some people find MCQ-type questions easier than others. If you find this part of the examination difficult then practice more MCQs to improve your technique.

Revision for MCQ-type questions

It would be comforting to read and learn a range of textbooks and articles and then feel confident about answering most of the questions. This is incredibly boring and time consuming! However, there are several methods to help you improve your scoring.

•   Practice as many MCQ-type questions as possible. A mock MCQ paper is found on page 112. Also see *MRCGP MCQ Practice Papers* by Peter Elliott published by PasTest.
•   Bear in mind the topic distribution and concentrate on these areas. It is well worth noting that questions on practice organisation (service management) are becoming increasingly common.
•   After working through an MCQ paper it quickly becomes obvious which areas are your 'black holes' — concentrate on these areas. Many topics will not require extensive revision since you will already have developed the knowledge base required at medical school and through various other medical experiences.

Final hints

- The best way to obtain a good mark is to have as wide a knowledge as possible of the topics being tested in the exam
- Read each question carefully and be sure you understand it
- Mark your responses clearly, correctly and accurately
- Use reasoning to work out the answers and guess at those you do not know
- Try to enjoy it and keep calm!

PRACTICE MULTIPLE CHOICE QUESTIONS

An index to the topics covered in these questions is given in Appendix 7.

The following factors have been positively linked with breast cancer:

1   onset of menstruation after 15 years of age
2   obesity
3   high alcohol consumption
4   low socio-economic status in developed countries
5   age over 30 years at birth of first child, provided there have been no previous incomplete pregnancies

A patient presents with a large swelling confined to the scrotum. It is transilluminable and the testis can be felt separately. The diagnosis may be

6   a hydrocele
7   an inguinal hernia
8   hydrocele of the cord
9   an epididymal cyst
10   epididymal tuberculosis

Familial adenomatous polyposis

11   may be inherited as an autosomal dominant condition
12   is pre-malignant
13   occurs in severe ulcerative colitis
14   may cause electrolyte disturbance
15   may be asymptomatic

Absolute contraindications to breast-feeding include

16   infants with galactosaemia
17   maternal tuberculosis
18   maternal HIV
19   atenolol
20   cytotoxic drugs

The peak expiratory flow rate

21   is increased in obstructive airways disease
22   is effort independent
23   is a suitable measurement to attempt on a three-year-old
24   is diagnostic of asthma if the value increases by 20% after
     administration of bronchodilators
25   is influenced by airway diameter

A result statistically significant at a level of 5% implies that

26   5% of the population are likely to agree with the result
27   the critical ratio is greater than or equal to 2.0
28   there is a 5% chance of the result being wrong
29   the coefficient of correlation (r) is 0.95
30   the result could not be accepted as valid

The following are true about somatization disorder:

31   onset occurs usually after 30 years of age
32   the condition is more common in men than in women
33   the course tends to be fluctuating but chronic
34   anxiety and depression occur frequently
35   menstrual dysfunction in women is common

Significant side-effects of selective serotonin re-uptake inhibitors (SSRIs) include

36   anorgasmia
37   insomnia
38   sweating
39   dystonia
40   retention of urine

Angioplasty

41   is ideal for treatment of a discrete stenosis of the main stem of the left coronary artery

42   is dangerous for patients with multiple vessel disease

43   is contraindicated in patients who have undergone bypass surgery

44   is contraindicated in patients with unstable angina

45   usually involves complications if there is acute occlusion of the lesion

The weaknesses of retrospective studies of the role of a suspected factor in the aetiology of a disease, as compared with prospective studies, are that

46   they are more costly and take longer

47   there may be bias in determining the presence or absence of a suspected factor

48   there may be bias in determining the presence or absence of the resulting disease

49   it is more difficult to obtain controls

50   it is more difficult to assure comparability of cases and controls

The following statements about benzodiazepines are true:

51   lorazepam has a longer duration of action than diazepam following a single dose

52   paradoxical disinhibition contraindicates continued use of benzodiazepines

53   nitrazepam is safe as a regularly prescribed hypnotic in the elderly

54   dependence is most likely with drugs that have a short elimination half-life

55   withdrawal symptoms are best treated with a sedative neuroleptic such as thioridazine

Impetigo

56   is contagious
57   is best treated with topical antibiotics
58   can cause a bullous rash
59   causes a fever in the majority of cases
60   is usually due to staphylococcal infection

The following are true of 'heartsink' patients:

61   the majority are women
62   they typically present with a single problem
63   they have higher referral rates than the average population
64   the average general practitioner is able to identify more than 50 such patients on his list
65   they have significantly more social problems than the average person

Following myocardial infarction the chances of recurrence can be reduced if the patient

66   stops smoking
67   is routinely started on an anti-arrhythmic drug
68   is started on a β-blocker
69   is started on daily low-dose aspirin
70   is started on a low cholesterol diet

The following statements are true of the HIV antibody test:

71   the interval between seroconversion and exposure to infection is usually no more than 2 months
72   a seronegative individual can infect other people
73   the virus is more readily isolated from blood than other body fluids
74   a positive antibody test is always indicative of infection
75   detection of antibodies is the cheapest and most accurate of HIV diagnostic procedures

Predictors of poor outcome in schizophrenia include

76   early onset
77   asocial premorbid personality
78   family history of affective disorder
79   clear consciousness
80   negative symptoms

Risk factors for congenital dislocation of the hip include

81   breech delivery
82   spina bifida
83   male sex
84   positive family history
85   being first born

Polymyalgia rheumatica characteristically

86   is associated with raised serum creatinine phosphokinase (CPK)
      levels
87   affects the shoulder girdles
88   is associated with morning stiffness
89   causes proximal muscle weakness
90   is readily diagnosed by muscle biopsy

In post-traumatic stress disorder the following are seen:

91   delusions
92   derealisation
93   guilt
94   flashbacks
95   irritability

Concerning child sexual abuse

96   it occurs in up to 10% of children
97   child sexual abusers often have a history of being abused as a child
98   girls are 20 times more likely to be abused than boys
99   it is associated with an increased incidence of anal fissures
100   reflex anal dilatation is pathognomonic

Ankylosing spondylitis

101   is as prevalent as rheumatoid arthritis
102   is associated with HLA-B27
103   improves with exercise
104   affects men more than women in a ratio of 10:1
105   is most unlikely if the ESR is normal

The following statements about pruritus are true:

106   cholestatic pruritus is probably due to an increase of bile
       salts in the skin
107   drugs which slow hepatic microsomal function may improve
       cholestatic pruritus
108   it is a common symptom of diabetes mellitus
109   it is a symptom of both hyperthyroidism and hypothyroidism
110   it is a recognised symptom of folate deficiency

Intracranial aneurysms

111   are linked to the presence of hypertension in a significant
       proportion of patients
112   are seldom familial
113   form most commonly on the anterior communicating artery
114   are multiple in over 50% of patients
115   occur most commonly in the age group 40—60

The following facts about the menopause are true:

116   it is due to loss of pituitary drive to the ovaries
117   up to 10% of cases of postmenopausal bleeding are due to
       malignancy
118   a premenopausal woman's risk of coronary artery disease is one
       fifth of that of a man of the same age
119   osteoclastic bone formation is slowed by the menopause
120   postmenopausal women at risk of osteoporosis should be
       encouraged to take calcium supplements

The following statements about traveller's diarrhoea are true:

121   the most common causative agent worldwide is *Giardia lamblia*
122   most infective agents are food and water borne
123   heating water to 50° C will kill most pathogens
124   water filters are no longer recommended because they frequently become colonised by bacteria
125   antimicrobials are rarely indicated

Characteristic features of endogenous depression include

126   incongruity of mood and thinking
127   early morning waking
128   failure to respond to chlorpromazine therapy
129   feelings of worthlessness
130   loss of libido

Helicobacter pylori

131   is a Gram-positive, flagellate bacillus
132   is found in the mucus that lines the gastric epithelium
133   is present in most patients with duodenal ulcer disease
134   is effectively eradicated by a two-week course of bismuth, metronidazole and tetracycline
135   should be eradicated in cases of gastric ulceration

Screening is available routinely in the UK for the relatives of patients with the following:

136   Tay-Sachs disease
137   Duchenne muscular dystrophy
138   Gilbert's syndrome
139   sickle cell disease
140   Wilson's disease

In carcinoma of the bronchus, the following suggest an inoperable lesion:

141   a paralysed hemidiaphragm
142   vocal cord palsy
143   pleural effusion
144   hypertrophic pulmonary osteoarthropathy
145   peripheral neuropathy

The following statements are correct:

146   coronary angioplasty is associated with a re-stenosis rate of
      30—40%
147   coronary artery bypass grafting improves survival in patients
      with single vessel coronary disease
148   use of the internal mammary artery for bypass grafting
      should be limited to patients in whom vein grafts are not
      available
149   coronary artery bypass grafting in uncomplicated cases is
      associated with an operative mortality of about 5%
150   aortic valve replacement should not be performed in patients
      with aortic stenosis and impaired left ventricular function
      because of an unacceptably high operative mortality

**The following make a non-organic cause of recurrent abdominal pain
more likely:**

151   a 3 year history
152   night pain
153   a family history of migraine
154   mouth ulceration
155   weight loss

Non-insulin dependent diabetes mellitus

156   is more prevalent than insulin-dependent diabetes mellitus in all
      populations
157   is a mild form of diabetes mellitus which reduces life
      expectancy only minimally
158   is seldom accompanied by macrovascular disease
159   is characterised by marked sensitivity to insulin action
160   can be successfully treated by dietary modification alone

The following are recognised features of hypothyroidism:

161   menorrhagia
162   ascites
163   cerebellar ataxia
164   clubbing
165   normochromic anaemia

Seborrhoeic warts

166   are always multiple
167   are pre-malignant in many cases
168   are infective
169   never occur on the palms or soles
170   have a recognised association with internal malignancy

The following are recognised clinical manifestations of myasthenia gravis:

171   wasting of proximal muscles
172   dysphagia
173   peripheral sensory loss
174   double vision
175   fluctuating symptoms

Complications of rubella infection include

176   orchitis
177   thrombocytopenic purpura
178   arthritis
179   encephalitis
180   congenital cataract

Tardive dyskinesia

181   is most common in the young
182   may occur when no medication has been taken
183   may be helped by benzodiazepines
184   may be helped by tetrabenazine
185   occurs in the first weeks of neuroleptic treatment

In a double-blind controlled study of the effect a new drug has on anxiety levels

186   patients are not told whether they are receiving a drug or a placebo
187   the doctor must know which tablet he is giving to his patients
188   a 'cross-over' technique can be used
189   only self-rated assessment can be used
190   observer-rated assessment of anxiety would suffice alone

The following statements about sulphonylureas are true:

191   they act by stimulating intracellular phosphorylation
192   the hypoglycaemic effectiveness usually stays constant over many years in most patients
193   some sulphonylureas can cause bone marrow depression
194   they are particularly effective in young, thin Type I diabetic patients
195   they should not be combined with biguanides

The following drugs should be avoided in hypertensive patients with the following conditions:

196   thiazide diuretics in patients with gout
197   calcium antagonists in patients with glucose intolerance
198   β-blockers in patients with cardiac failure
199   calcium antagonists in patients with ischaemic heart disease
200   β-blockers in patients with obstructive airways disease

Volatile substance abuse

201   may involve butane and propane
202   occurs at some point in about 5% of 15-year-old children in the UK
203   in most children lasts less than 6 months
204   is more common among girls than boys
205   can cause renal failure

The following facts about duodenal ulceration are true:

206   virtually all patients with duodenal ulcers are colonized by *H. pylori*

207   eradication of *H. pylori* leads to the healing of duodenal ulcers but has no effect on the incidence of ulcer relapse

208   duodenal ulcers do not occur in anacidic patients

209   patients with duodenal ulcer secrete no more acid, on average, than healthy people

210   patients with duodenal ulcer occur more commonly in urban than in rural populations

In the Mental Health Act 1983

211   Section 4 deals with emergency admissions for up to 72 hours

212   Section 2 requires a second, approved, doctor to complete the form

213   an approved social worker is essential for the completion of a Section 2 admission

214   if a general practitioner's partner is an 'approved doctor' he is allowed to act as the second doctor to complete any necessary forms

215   to arrange a Section 4 admission, the doctor must have examined the patient within the previous 3 days

School refusal

216   is different from truancy

217   is commonly associated with physical symptoms

218   is associated with anxiety and depression

219   can be treated with antidepressants

220   generally has a poor outcome

The following conditions cause unilateral blindness of rapid onset:

221   detachment of retina

222   central retinal artery embolism

223   vitreous haemorrhage

224   retinitis pigmentosa

225   retrobulbar neuritis

Breast-feeding reduces the incidence of

226   atopy in infants born to mothers with a history of atopy
227   gastrointestinal infection
228   nappy rash
229   respiratory infection
230   infantile colic

Concerning undescended testis

231   it is more common in premature infants
232   by 12 months 5% remain outside the scrotum
233   orchidopexy can be safely left until the second decade
234   there is an increased risk of infertility
235   there is an increased risk of malignant change

Recognised symptoms in irritable bowel syndrome include

236   a sense of incomplete defaecation
237   passage of mucus per rectum
238   rectal bleeding
239   a sense of abdominal distension
240   loss of weight

In a normal distribution

241   95% of the population lie within two standard deviations of both sides of the mean
242   68% of the population lie within two standard deviations of the mean
243   the mean is equal in value to the mode
244   the median is equal in value to the mode
245   the standard deviation is equal to the variance

The following factors would suggest an increased risk of suicide in depressed patients:

246   co-existing problems of alcohol abuse
247   history of aggressive behaviour
248   co-existing chronic physical illness
249   living in a rural environment
250   married status

Oestrogen replacement therapy in menopausal women is more effective than a placebo in relieving

251   depression
252   insomnia
253   poor memory
254   anxiety
255   palpitations

Factors that increase the risk of suicide include

256   advancing age
257   social class I
258   the presence of hopelessness
259   antisocial personality disorder
260   talking about suicidal ideas

Client-centred psychotherapy

261   is interpretive
262   was developed by Rogers
263   is directive
264   is non-judgemental
265   aims principally at the subject gaining insight

The aim of a gluten-free diet is to exclude the proteins of

266   oats
267   wheat
268   barley
269   maize
270   rye

The following apply to infectious diseases:

271   since 1992 there has been a reduction in the incidence of
           Haemophilus influenzae type B infections in children
272   there has been a general decline in the number of confirmed
           cases of measles since 1994
273   smallpox was declared to have been eradicated from the world
           in the 1960s
274   *H. influenzae* type B organisms are subject to antigenic shift
275   approximately 90% of adults are immune to chickenpox

The following are signs of a parietal lobe lesion:

276   grasp reflex
277   emotional lability
278   homonymous quadrantanopia
279   sensory inattention
280   difficulty calculating numbers

Concerning sudden infant death syndrome

281   prematurity is a risk factor
282   the risk is increased with increasing maternal age
283   it is more common in females
284   it is associated with paternal smoking
285   it is associated with sleeping on plastic mattresses

In retinal vein occlusion

286   glaucoma is an important risk factor
287   the onset of symptoms usually occurs within minutes
288   there are characteristic haemorrhages in the affected sector of
           the retina
289   subsequent improvement in vision is rare
290   aspirin is indicated for long-term prophylaxis

A low serum B12 is associated with

291 a total gastrectomy
292 phenytoin therapy
293 pregnancy
294 Addisonian pernicious anaemia
295 cirrhosis of the liver

The following are characteristic of toxic shock syndrome:

296 multi-system involvement
297 isolation, often in pure culture, of anaerobic streptococci
298 occurrence predominantly in females
299 hypotension
300 a macular rash followed by desquamation of palms and soles

The following statements about asbestosis are true:

301 the first signs of asbestosis usually occur 2 to 3 years following exposure
302 pleural plaques are the most common radiological sign of exposure to asbestos
303 following diagnosis, active treatment with chest physiotherapy is required
304 heavy exposure to asbestos is normally necessary to cause asbestosis
305 fine end-inspiratory crackles at the lung bases are a reliable sign of asbestosis

Diabetic microalbuminuria

306 occurs within 10 years of diabetes
307 is a predictor of early cardiovascular mortality in type II diabetes
308 is best assessed by a timed collection during the day
309 is not affected by improved glycaemic control
310 when accompanied by hypertension is best treated with ACE inhibitors

Mesalazine compounds

311 are useful in the maintenance of remission of ulcerative colitis
312 have no value in the treatment of active small bowel Crohn's disease
313 are contraindicated in pregnancy
314 may cause impotence
315 can be given by enema

In adult polycystic kidney disease

316 patients are always hypertensive
317 there may be cysts in the pancreas and the liver
318 haematuria is a recognised feature
319 transplantation is contraindicated
320 there is an association with medullary sponge kidney

In colorectal cancer

321 there is a correlation between the consumption of meat and animal fat and the likelihood of developing cancer of the colon
322 faecal occult blood testing will detect 90% of cases
323 there is an increased incidence of rectal tumours in beer drinkers
324 the adenomatous polyposis coli (APC) gene maps to chromosome 2
325 hereditary non-polyposis colon cancer accounts for up to a third of all cases of colon cancer

Concerning influenza immunisation

326 anaphylactic hypersensitivity to egg protein is a contraindication
327 routine immunisation of health care workers is recommended
328 the vaccine is live
329 the vaccine is given by intradermal injection
330 cystic fibrosis is a contraindication

Paralysis of the left 3rd cranial nerve causes

331   constricted pupil on the left
332   ptosis on the left
333   normal direct light reflex on the left
334   absence of sweating on the left side of the face
335   inability to abduct the left eye

Recognised features of Reiter's syndrome include

336   balanitis xerotica obliterans
337   calcaneal spurs
338   posterior uveitis
339   sacroiliitis
340   subungual keratosis

Infectious mononucleosis

341   is most conveniently and cheaply diagnosed by the Paul-Bunnell test
342   is more severe in children than in adults
343   should be treated with aspirin in adolescents
344   spreads characteristically in epidemics rather than on a sporadic,
      case by case basis
345   is characterised by night sweats and swinging fevers which may rise
      to 40° C

In thyroid cancer

346   hyperthyroidism is often present
347   anaplastic lesions typically occur in the young
348   there is characteristically a 'hot nodule' on radioisotope scanning
      of the thyroid gland
349   bone metastases are exceptional
350   the papillary type carries a better prognosis than the follicular type

In migrainous neuralgia (cluster headache)

351   the attacks tend to occur at night
352   the pain is always unilateral
353   the pain commonly lasts up to 12 hours
354   there may be ptosis on the affected side
355   the attacks may be precipitated by alcohol

A child of 3 years would be expected to

356   copy a square
357   name two colours
358   ride a tricycle
359   go upstairs one foot per step
360   build a tower of six cubes

An undescended testis

361   should be brought into the scrotum after the age of 10 years
362   is rarely associated with an inguinal hernia
363   is prone to malignant change
364   is more likely to undergo torsion than a normal testis
365   means that the patient will be sterile

The following factors predispose to major depression:

366   social groups A and B
367   a first degree relative with major depression
368   the presence of more than 3 children in the home
369   employment in the same company for more than 10 years
370   loss of a parent before 11 years of age

Recognised features of depression in the elderly include

371   delusions of poverty
372   pseudodementia
373   a strong association with bereavement
374   agitated movements
375   retarded movements

Where an association between two variables is said to be statistically significant

376   reliability and validity are proven
377   the association is likely to occur by chance only at a pre-determined level of probability
378   a causal association has been established
379   if repeated, the chances are the results of the association would be the same
380   it implies that $p < 0.1$

General practitioners

381   are responsible for any errors made by their practice nurse
382   are responsible for care of their patients at all times
383   are obliged to order any drug (that does not appear on the black list) for the treatment of a patient on an NHS prescription form
384   are responsible for errors made by a spouse when answering the telephone
385   if complaints are made against them the most probable reason is failure to refer to hospital

Spontaneous rib fracture may be caused by

386   coughing
387   metastases
388   primary lung tumour
389   pneumothorax
390   osteoporosis

The following have been proven to improve the outcome of embolic stroke:

391   heparin
392   warfarin therapy in the presence of atrial fibrillation
393   attention to pressure areas by regular turning
394   carotid end-arterectomy if a carotid bruit is present
395   MRI scan

Dark urine occurs with

396 beetroot consumption
397 heavy proteinuria
398 porphyria
399 malaria
400 Gilbert's syndrome

Multiple sclerosis is likely to run a relatively benign course if

401 onset is at an early age
402 onset is with optic neuritis
403 onset is with cerebellar lesions
404 complete recovery from an episode occurs
405 onset is with sensory symptoms

A femoral hernia

406 is more common in females
407 usually disappears on lying down
408 is unlikely to become strangulated
409 is often asymptomatic unless it becomes complicated
410 has a neck below the inguinal ligament

On issuing a prescription for a controlled drug, the doctor must

411 write the whole script, including patient's name and address, in his own handwriting
412 write the dose in words and figures
413 keep a copy of the script in the patient's notes
414 specify the pharmacy where it is to be dispensed
415 notify the Home Office Drugs Branch if he suspects that the person is addicted to such drugs

Bacterial vaginosis

416 is caused by *Gardnerella vaginalis*
417 is characterised by intense vaginal wall inflammation
418 is characterised by an unpleasant odour and persistent pruritus
419 is commonly treated with metronidazole
420 rarely recurs following successful treatment

Recognised features of anorexia nervosa include

421   increased plasma cortisol
422   frequent structural abnormalities of the hypothalamus
423   male hypersexuality
424   hypokalaemia
425   total loss of body hair

In a study of patients with seizures, 50 patients had EEGs performed, of which 30 had abnormalities. 10% of normal people have EEG abnormalities. The following statements are true:

426   the specificity is 62%
427   the specificity is 5%
428   the value of the EEG in detecting seizures depends on the prevalence of seizures
429   the positive predictive value is 75%
430   if the prevalence of seizures in the population is 5%, and 1,000 persons are screened in a month, the number of false positives will be 30

The following features suggest a normal bereavement reaction rather than depressive illness:

431   complaints of physical symptoms
432   emotional numbness
433   suicidal thoughts
434   searching behaviour
435   feelings of worthlessness

Recognised side effects of treatment with omeprazole include

436   gynaecomastia
437   erythema multiforme
438   headache
439   bradycardia
440   pancreatitis

Concerning emergency contraception

441   an intrauterine contraceptive device must be inserted within 3 days of coitus to be effective
442   insertion of an intrauterine contraceptive device has been shown to be more effective than hormonal methods
443   failed hormonal contraception is an indication for termination of pregnancy on the grounds of teratogenic risk
444   established breast-feeding is a contraindication to hormonal postcoital contraception
445   surveys have shown that approximately 50% of women are unaware of postcoital methods of contraception

Chronic simple glaucoma

446   is the commonest type of glaucoma
447   is more common in whites than in blacks
448   is of unknown pathology
449   causes peripheral visual loss
450   should be diagnosed primarily on the basis of intraocular pressure measurements

In osteoporosis

451   thyrotoxicosis may be a cause
452   serum alkaline phosphatase may be raised above normal levels
453   serum osteocalcin is a marker of bone formation
454   treatment with biphosphonates may prevent vertebral fractures
455   bone density should be monitored at 6 monthly intervals in severe disease

Concerning vesico-ureteric reflux

456   it may remain clinically silent until adulthood
457   it may present with nausea and vomiting
458   it is usually associated with coliform urinary tract infection
459   ureteric reimplantation is of no value
460   the prophylactic antibiotic of choice is ampicillin

A lump in the midline of the neck may be a

461 dermoid cyst
462 sebaceous cyst
463 thyroglossal cyst
464 branchial cyst
465 cystic hygroma

The following agents have been shown to reduce mortality significantly after myocardial infarction:

466 captopril
467 nifedipine
468 oral nitrates
469 timolol
470 simvastatin

In red eye

471 conjunctivitis is a likely diagnosis if there is an accompanying sticky discharge
472 episcleritis is a serious condition that needs prompt treatment
473 iritis presents with the redness mostly around the cornea
474 keratitis is particularly associated with rheumatoid arthritis
475 acute glaucoma may be intensely painful

Hypercalcaemia may be caused by

476 Addison's disease
477 multiple myeloma
478 hyperthyroidism
479 Paget's disease
480 vitamin D intoxication

In schizophrenia

481   the age of onset is on average 5 years earlier in females
482   the outcome is better in developed compared with developing countries
483   the risk of developing the disorder is higher amongst lower social class families
484   the 'expressed emotion' of close family members is predictive of relapse
485   functional deterioration usually continues insidiously over the whole illness course

The following factors increase the risk of psychiatric sequelae to head injury:

486   prolonged retrograde amnesia
487   a family history of mental disorder
488   the complete absence of post-traumatic amnesia
489   younger age
490   where the circumstances of the injury prohibit compensation

Specific contraindications to routine primary vaccination include

491   immunosuppressive therapy
492   infantile eczema
493   first trimester of pregnancy
494   under six months of age
495   during an epidemic

The following are recognised features of Down's syndrome:

496   coarctation of the aorta
497   secundum atrial septal defect
498   early development of Alzheimer's disease
499   increased prevalence of atherosclerosis
500   deletion of chromosome 15q 11-13

PRACTICE MULTIPLE CHOICE QUESTION ANSWERS

1:False 2:True 3:True 4:False 5:False

Case-control studies suggest that the risk of breast cancer for women whose menarche occurs before they are 12 years old is almost double that for women who begin menstruating after the age of 13 years. The rapid establishment of regular menstruation increases the risk. High socio-economic class in developed countries is linked with breast cancer, as is early age at birth of first child. Incomplete pregnancies do not seem to provide a protective effect.

6:False 7:False 8:True 9:True 10:False

A hydrocele envelops the testis and the testis is usually not palpable. A strangulated inguinal hernia may occur in the scrotum but does not transilluminate. An encysted hydrocele of the cord in the scrotum is separate from the testis and transilluminates. An epididymal cyst is fluid filled and separate from the testis. Therefore the testis is palpable separately. Epididymal tuberculosis causes swelling confined to the scrotum; there is thickening of the cord which feels hard. It does not transilluminate.

11:True 12:True 13:False 14:True 15:True

Familial adenomatous polyposis (FAP) is an autosomal dominant inherited condition. It is characterised by multiple polyps throughout the colon and rectum. It develops in teenage years when it is initially asymptomatic and benign. Later, symptoms develop and patients present with a change in bowel habit, i.e. loose stools, rectal bleeding and mucus per rectum. Malignant change inevitably occurs within 20 years. Prophylactic surgery is the treatment of choice with total colectomy and ileorectal anastomosis or pouch-anal anastomosis. In ulcerative colitis, inflammatory polyps may occur, but this is not the inherited condition FAP. Electrolyte disturbance occurs when there is considerable loss of mucus and blood per rectum.

16:True 17:False 18:False 19:False 20:True

Contraindications to breast-feeding are either absolute (always apply) or relative.

Absolute contraindications
Galactosaemia
Cytotoxic (immunosuppressive) drugs e.g. methotrexate, cyclophosphamide
Relative contraindications
Tuberculosis
Hepatitis B
Chickenpox
Maternal ill health
Amiodarone
Atenolol
Ergot alkaloids
Gold salts
Radiopharmaceuticals
With regard to tuberculosis, infants can be immunised at birth with isoniazid resistant BCG and treated with a course of isoniazid. With regard to HIV, the virus has been cultured from breast milk and is transmitted in it. In the Western world this makes breast-feeding contraindicated as it will increase the perinatal transmission rate. The problem is not so straightforward in the developing world where the risks associated with bottle-feeding are high.

21:False 22:False 23:False 24:True 25:True

The peak expiratory flow rate is the maximum expiratory flow rate following a full inspiration. It is dependent upon the diameter of the airways at the narrowest point and the intra-thoracic pressure generated. It is effort dependent. Very few children under the age of 5 years can do a peak flow. The forced expiratory volume (FEV_1) is the volume of air that can be forcibly expired in one second. It is less effort dependent and more reproducible than the peak expiratory flow rate. In asthma the residual volume will increase, reducing the forced vital capacity.

26:False 27:True 28:True 29:False 30:False

'Statistically significant' implies a critical ratio greater than or equal to 2.0. This is equivalent to a level of significance greater than or equal to 5%, i.e. the likelihood of a standard deviation being >2 or <2 by chance is about 5 in 100. In a psychological study this level of significance would normally be accepted as valid, although a higher or lower level could be used if wished.

31:False 32:False 33:True 34:True 35:True

Somatization disorder is a chronic syndrome of multiple somatic symptoms that cannot be explained medically. It is associated with psychosocial distress and medical help-seeking. Diagnosis requires a history of several years duration. The onset occurs in early adulthood and rarely after 30 years of age. The belief that a person has been sickly most of their life is common. It is more common in women, affecting 1—2% of all females. Interpersonal problems are prominent with anxiety and depression being the most prevalent psychiatric conditions. Menstrual symptoms, sexual indifference and frigidity, alcohol and drug abuse and antisocial personality disorder all occur more frequently. Whilst the disorder fluctuates, patients are rarely symptom free.

36:True 37:True 38:True 39:True 40:False

SSRIs are effective antidepressants with less sedative effect than tricyclics, few antimuscarinic effects and low cardiotoxicity. The most frequent side-effects are gastrointestinal (diarrhoea, nausea and vomiting) which are dose related. Restlessness, anxiety, insomnia and sweating may be marked initially. Side-effects also include anorexia, weight loss and allergic reactions including anaphylaxis (all more common with fluoxetine), convulsions (particularly with fluvoxamine), extrapyramidal reactions and a withdrawal syndrome (particularly with paroxetine), abnormalities of hepatic enzymes (particularly with fluvoxamine and sertraline) and sexual dysfunction including anorgasmia and ejaculatory failure in males (particularly with paroxetine and fluoxetine).

41:False 42:False 43:False 44:False 45:True

The left main stem is not suitable for angioplasty because occlusion during attempted angioplasty might be catastrophic. Multiple vessel angioplasty is now commonplace. Previous bypass surgery is not a contraindication to angioplasty, which may offer fewer risks than repeat surgery. The treatment of unstable angina may account for 25—30% of procedures in some centres.

46:False 47:True 48:False 49:False 50:False

Although time consuming, a cohort study allows for determination of a population-based rate of the event under question. A case-control study, on the other hand, is relatively easy and inexpensive to conduct since long-term follow-up is not required. In a cohort study, potential bias is lessened because exposure can be determined prior to the onset of disease, whereas with a case-control study, there is potential for bias in the selection of subjects since a case-control study is not population based. The incidence rate of an event or disease for exposed and non-exposed populations can be calculated for a cohort study. Causality cannot be determined for either a case-control or a cohort study.

51:True 52:False 53:False 54:True 55:False

Lorazepam, a 'short-acting' benzodiazepine, has a longer distribution half-life (HLD) and thus a longer sedative effect following a single dose, but no active metabolites and a shorter elimination half-life (HLE 10—20 hours) compared with the 'long-acting' benzodiazepine diazepam (HLE 30—100 hours). The HLE of nitrazepam, usually 18—36 hours, is longer in the elderly leading to drug accumulation, confusion, ataxia, falls and increased mortality. Paradoxical disinhibition may be treated with a dose reduction or increase. Dependence is increased by high doses, dose escalation, prolonged treatment, high potency drugs, drugs with a short HLE, and in patients with dependent personality traits. Withdrawal symptoms are best treated with a gradual reducing regime using a long-acting benzodiazepine.

56:True 57:False 58:True 59:False 60:True

Impetigo can be classified as simple (non-bullous) or bullous. Bullae are usually flaccid, rupture easily and contain pus. The usual infecting agent is *Staphylococcus aureus*. The lesions occur in clusters, are usually found at the extremities and are highly infectious. Non-bullous impetigo is due to either *Staphylococcus aureus* or group A beta haemolytic streptococcus. Lesions are painless and not usually associated with systemic symptoms. Regional adenitis can occur. Topical antibiotics are not generally helpful and systemic antibiotics are the treatment of choice. Erythromycin or penicillin and flucloxacillin should be used.

61:True 62:False 63:False 64:False 65:True

Currently in vogue is the term 'heartsink patient'; they are difficult to define and are not always frequent attenders. GPs usually contain such patients within the practice and do not refer elsewhere. The average doctor has 20—30 such patients and examining their medical record folders reveals a variety of different diagnoses at each consultation. They also have significantly more psychological, social and family problems.

66:True 67:False 68:True 69:True 70:False

Anti-arrhythmic drugs are not routinely recommended following myocardial infarction. They may not be effective against ventricular infarction. They may not be effective against ventricular fibrillation and some can induce arrhythmias themselves. β-blockers undoubtedly reduce fatality, although appropriate dosage is in doubt for some. The simplest to use is timolol 5 mg b.d. increasing to 10 mg b.d. for a maximum of 2 years. Aspirin in the dose 150—160 mg/day is beneficial.

71:True 72:True 73:True 74:False 75:True

General epidemiological data suggest that the interval between HIV exposure and seroconversion is usually no more than 2 months, and this justifies setting a 3—6 month limit to the follow-up of individuals who have been sexually exposed to HIV infection. Antibody status usually, but not always, indicates the ability of an individual to infect other people; for example, there are several instances of HIV transmission by blood donations from seronegative donors. False-positive antibody tests are not uncommon so all positive results must be cross-checked.

76:True 77:True 78:False 79:True 80:True

Factors predictive of a poor outcome and chronic course in schizophrenia include:
- an early age of onset
- low socio-economic status
- regular occupational record
- social adversity
- a family history of schizophrenia
- schizoid or asocial premorbid personality traits
- low intelligence
- lack of a lasting heterosexual relationship
- absence of precipitating factors
- insidious onset
- longer duration of untreated psychosis
- lack of clouding of consciousness or confusion
- absence of a family history of affective disorder or an affective
  component to the illness
- presence of primary negative symptoms
- neurological signs and symptoms
- a history of perinatal trauma.

81:True 82:True 83:False 84:True 85:True

Risk factors for congenital dislocation of the hip:
- family history (positive in 20%)
- female sex (female:male, 6:1)
- breech delivery (factor in 30%)
- spina bifida
- being first born
- oligohydramnios
- the left hip is more likely to be dislocated than the right.
Ultrasound is the best test for diagnosis.
The clinical tests of hip instability are Ortolani's and Barlow's.

86:False 87:True 88:True 89:False 90:False

In polymyalgia rheumatica the proximal muscles ache, are stiff and, in
the mornings, may be tender, but are not genuinely weak. The serum
CPK, electromyogram (EMG) and muscle biopsy are all normal.
Diagnosis is based on the clinical features and usually the ESR is
markedly elevated.

91:False 92:True 93:True 94:True 95:True

Shell-shock and combat neurosis are alternative names. The patient displays guilty ideation but not of delusional intensity.

96:True 97:True 98:False 99:True 100:False

Child sexual abuse occurs when a person who is sexually mature involves the child in any activity which the other person expects to lead to their own sexual arousal. This includes exposure, pornography, sexual acts with the child and masturbation. The prevalence suggested by a MORI poll in adults asking whether they had been abused as children (UK, 1985) is approximately 10%; this is probably an underestimate. 12% of females and 8% of males reported abuse. About 60% of child sexual abuse is by an immediate family member. There is often a history of generational abuse. There is a current conviction rate of abusers taken to court of 5%. The court cases are extremely distressing to the child, as they may be accused of lying or feel that they have not been believed if conviction does not occur. The worry about not being believed is probably one reason for lack of disclosure in school age children who have been sexually abused.

Child sexual abusers often have a history of child sexual abuse (approximately 27% sexually abused as a child and 17% witnessed child sexual abuse) but this does not mean that all children who are abused go on to abuse.

Facts about abusers

4% mothers
7% baby sitters
10% older brothers
17% unrelated men (who may be part of an organised paedophile ring).
31% fathers

Anal fissures are common in children who are sexually abused. In children who are sexually abused there is an increased incidence of anorexia, headaches, recurrent abdominal pain, encopresis, enuresis and behavioural problems. There is a higher prevalence of child sexual abuse in children with special educational needs. Reflex anal dilatation is not a normal reflex. It may occur in inflammatory bowel disease, in chronic constipation, with the use of enemas and after anal stretch surgery, but it also occurs after anal penetration. The conclusion of the Cleveland Inquiry (1988) was that '... the sign of anal dilatation is abnormal and suspicious and requires further investigation. It is not in itself evidence of anal abuse.'

Strong indicators of child sexual abuse are pregnancy, sexually transmitted disease, lacerations or scars in the hymen, anal fissures and positive forensic tests (semen). Child sexual abuse is associated with physical abuse in 15% of cases.

101:True 102:True 103:True 104:False 105:False

Ankylosing spondylitis was once considered an uncommon disease but it is now known to have a similar prevalence to rheumatoid arthritis. It was also thought to affect males predominantly but recent studies have shown a comparable distribution between the sexes. Elevation of the ESR occurs in 50% of patients but may be normal despite severe disease.

106:True 107:False 108:False 109:True 110:False

Cholestatic pruritus may be improved by drugs that speed hepatic microsomal function (such as phenobarbitone). Pruritus is reported in as few as 1% of diabetics. Iron deficiency (rather than folate deficiency) may cause pruritus which in turn responds to iron therapy.

111:False 112:True 113:False 114:False 115:True

Hypertension does not appear to be a significant factor in the formation of intracranial aneurysms, but women who smoke are two and a half times more likely to develop aneurysmal subarachnoid haemorrhage than non-smokers. About 90% of aneurysms develop in the anterior communicating, internal carotid and middle cerebral arteries. Multiple aneurysms occur in only about 50% of patients.

116:False 117:True 118:True 119:False 120:False

The menopause is accompanied by a depletion of ovarian oocytes accompanied by a fall in oestrogen production which causes a rise in pituitary hormones, LH and FSH. Osteoclasts are responsible for bone resorption (not formation) and their activity is accelerated by the menopause, for reasons not understood. Calcium supplements appear to have a minor effect on cortical bone loss and no effect on trabecular bone, where osteoporosis is most likely to occur.

121:False 122:True 123:False 124:False 125:False

The most common causative agent of traveller's diarrhoea is *Escherichia coli*. Heating water to 100° C is necessary to kill most pathogens. Water filters retain a useful function and are widely recommended in developing countries. Short courses of empirical antimicrobials, for example ciprofloxacin, can be useful for traveller's diarrhoea, particularly for patients with underlying disease.

126:False 127:True 128:False 129:True 130:True

In endogenous depression, there is persistent depression of mood, unreactive to circumstances. Characteristic symptoms include early morning waking, morning worsening of mood, feelings of guilt or worthlessness with decline in concentration, energy, appetite, interest and libido. Although tricyclic antidepressants and electroconvulsive therapy (ECT) are the treatments of choice, some cases, especially when agitation and/or delusions are present, respond to chlorpromazine alone. Affective incongruity is a feature of schizophrenia.

131:False 132:True 133:True 134:True 135:False

Helicobacter pylori is a Gram-negative bacterium. It is found in 90% of duodenal ulcers and 70% of gastric ulcer disease, and is found in the mucus of the gastric epithelium as well as in areas of gastric metaplasia in the duodenum. It remains unclear whether eradication of *H. pylori* reduces the relapse rate in gastric ulceration.

136:True 137:True 138:False 139:True 140:True

In the UK, carrier screening is only undertaken for haemoglobinopathies, Tay-Sachs disease, thalassaemia and sickle cell disease. However, screening can be performed, if available, for Duchenne muscular dystrophy and Wilson's disease.

141:True 142:True 143:True 144:False 145:False

A paralysed hemidiaphragm and vocal cord palsy suggest mediastinal involvement by a tumour, with damage to phrenic and recurrent laryngeal nerves respectively. In theory an effusion may be secondary to a pneumonia distal to an occluding but operable carcinoma. In practice it almost invariably implies pleural involvement by tumour or blockage of lymphatic drainage by tumour in mediastinal glands. 144 and 145 are non-metastatic manifestations of malignant disease, and may regress with removal of the tumour.

146:True 147:False 148:False 149:False 150:False

Coronary angioplasty is associated with restenosis in 30—40% of cases and usually occurs in the first 3 months. Coronary artery bypass grafting (CABG) has been shown to improve survival in patients with triple vessel disease and impaired LV function, and in those with triple vessel disease with proximal left anterior descending artery involvement. Internal mammary artery grafts are preferable to saphenous vein grafts as they have greater long-term patency rate. CABG is associated with an overall mortality of 1—2%. All patients should be considered for valve replacement in aortic stenosis regardless of the degree of LV impairment.

151:True 152:False 153:True 154:False 155:False

Recurrent abdominal pain is very common in childhood affecting up to 10% of the school age population. In the majority of cases the aetiology is non-organic. The condition is more common in girls than in boys and a family history is common. The pain is usually peri-umbilical and rarely associated with other gastrointestinal symptoms such as diarrhoea, blood per rectum or weight loss. Abdominal pain accompanied by other symptoms is suggestive of organic pathology. Night pain is suggestive of oesophagitis or peptic ulceration. Diarrhoea with blood per rectum suggests a colitis and diarrhoea associated with weight loss malabsorption syndrome.

156:True 157:False 158:False 159:False 160:True

Non-insulin dependent diabetes (NIDDM) adversely affects both length and quality of life due to serious complications. The reduction in life expectancy averages 5—10 years in middle-aged patients with NIDDM. Macrovascular complications are frequently observed, regardless of age at diagnosis. Most patients demonstrate resistance to insulin action and may have high fasting levels although these are still lower than would be found in weight-matched normal subjects with similar plasma glucose levels.

161:True 162:True 163:True 164:False 165:True

Menorrhagia and normochromic anaemia are not uncommon complications of hypothyroidism. Macrocytosis and iron-deficiency anaemia are also well-recognised complications. Clinically significant ascites and cerebellar ataxia are rare. Clubbing and pretibial myxoedema are rare complications of thyrotoxicosis and, if seen, occur in conjunction with exophthalmos in thyroid acropathy.

166:False 167:False 168:False 169:True 170:True

Seborrhoeic warts may occur in any area where there are pilosebaceous follicles but are seen predominantly on the face or trunk and may be solitary. They undergo malignant change rarely, but an eruption of warts may be precipitated by an inflammatory dermatosis or by internal malignancy. They are non-infective.

171:False 172:True 173:False 174:True 175:True

Myasthenia gravis is characterised by abnormal fatiguability of muscles. The predilection is for ocular muscles and others of cranial nerve innervation. Ptosis, strabismus, double vision, dysarthria and dysphagia are common. The symptoms tend to fluctuate, the weakness being aggravated by repeated use of the muscle. Muscular wasting and sensory deficits are not seen in myasthenia gravis.

176:False 177:True 178:True 179:True 180:True

Transmission of rubella is by droplet spread. The incubation period is 14—21 days. Infection can be asymptomatic. Infection is now rare as a consequence of the immunisation programme. Prodromal symptoms may or may not be present and precede the rash by 1—5 days. These include fever, coryza, conjunctivitis and lymphadenopathy (sub-occipital, post auricular and cervical). The rash is macular and lasts for 3—5 days. Complications include persistent lymphadenopathy, arthritis, neuritis, thrombocytopenic purpura and encephalitis (associated with a CSF lymphocytosis).

Differential diagnosis of rubella:
- infectious mononucleosis
- toxoplasmosis
- enteroviral infection
- roseola, scarlet fever
- *Mycoplasma*
- parvovirus infection
- viral isolation is difficult and diagnosis is by serology.

Treatment is supportive. Prevention is by immunisation with the MMR vaccine.

Congenital rubella occurs secondary to maternal infection in the first trimester.

Clinical manifestations are variable and include:
- jaundice
- thrombocytopenia
- growth retardation
- cardiac abnormalities
- eye problems (cataracts, blindness, microphthalmia)
- deafness
- microcephaly
- fetal death
- stillbirth.

181:False 182:True 183:False 184:True 185:False

Tardive dyskinesia is more common in the elderly, may be idiopathic, may be helped by store-depleting neuroleptics, (but not benzodiazepines), and usually occurs only after prolonged treatment with neuroleptics.

186:True 187:False 188:True 189:False 190:False

In a double-blind trial neither the patients nor the doctor know which tablets are being given, by using a placebo and numbering the tablets. Estimation of anxiety would ideally include self- and observer-rated assessment.

166

191:False 192:False 193:True 194:False 195:False

The mechanism of action of sulphonylureas is not wholly clear. In part they stimulate insulin secretion from beta cells in the pancreas. The hypoglycaemic effectiveness of sulphonylureas often decreases with time. About 30% of diabetics on these drugs will be transferred to insulin within 4 years. Sulphonylureas are relatively contraindicated in young, thin type I patients, particularly if they are ketotic. There is no recognised benefit from combining sulphonylureas with biguanides.

196:True 197:False 198:True 199:False 200:True

Thiazide diuretics are contraindicated in patients with glucose intolerance, but not calcium antagonists. Calcium antagonists (or β-blockers) are indicated for hypertensive patients with ischaemic heart disease.

201:True 202:True 203:True 204:False 205:True

The peak age group for volatile substance abuse is 13—15 years, with boys outnumbering girls 4:1. Abuse usually lasts less than 6 months, but about 10% of abusers become dependent and some will progress to illicit drugs and alcohol.

206:True 207:False 208:True 209:False 210:True

It is now recognised that the strongest aetiological factor for duodenal ulcer is infection of the gastroduodenal mucosa with *H. pylori*. Not only does eradication of the *H. pylori* lead to healing of the duodenal ulcer, but it also causes a dramatic reduction in the incidence of ulcer relapse. *H. pylori* is also associated with other gastrointestinal diseases including chronic gastritis, gastric ulceration and gastric cancer. Duodenal ulcers do not occur in anacidic patients, just as they almost invariably occur in the presence of gross hypersecretion of acid as in the Zollinger-Ellison syndrome. Patients with duodenal ulcers secrete more acid on average than healthy controls and have also been found to have more parietal cells.

211:True 212:True 213:False 214:False 215:False

For Section 2 admissions a separate (not in the same partnership) and 'approved' doctor must complete the form. In Section 4 admissions the completing doctor must have examined the patient during the previous 24 hours.

216:True 217:True 218:True 219:True 220:False

School refusal is due to an excessive degree of anxiety making it difficult for the child to attend school. It occurs in about 1—2% of children of school age. There is equal sex incidence. It is most common at age 5—6 years and 11 years when a new school is started. Depression is present in about 50—70% of cases. Physical symptoms are common. The outcome is very good with a programme of psychotherapy and flooding therapy (taking the child to school, often under supervision of the therapist). Drug therapy is not indicated in most cases, but tricyclic antidepressants, e.g. imipramine, have been shown to be of use when there is co-existent depression. Truancy is differentiated from school refusal as it is the wilful avoidance of school and not due to anxiety about school attendance.

221:False 222:True 223:True 224:False 225:True

Central retinal artery occlusion, from embolus or arteritis, causes sudden complete and irreversible loss of vision. Retrobulbar neuritis results in pain and temporary loss of vision. Vitreous haemorrhage, which complicates diabetic proliferative retinopathy, may be so large that effective vision is suddenly lost. Retinal detachment usually causes progressive, but not necessarily rapid, loss of part of the visual field. Retinitis pigmentosa is a primary retinal degeneration that produces gradual but progressive loss of vision.

226:True 227:True 228:False 229:True 230:False

10% of the protein in mature breast milk is secretory IgA. Lymphocytes, macrophages, proteins with non-specific anti-bacterial activity and complement are also present. There have been many studies in the Third World to show that infants fed formula milk have a higher mortality and morbidity, particularly from gastrointestinal infection.

In the UK, studies have been done which show:
• breast-feeding for more than 13 weeks reduces the incidence of gastrointestinal and respiratory infections
• the response to immunisation with the HIB vaccine is higher in breast-fed infants than in formula fed infants
• the risk of necrotising enterocolitis in low birth weight babies is lower in those who are breast-fed.

The incidence of atopic eczema in infants born to atopic mothers is reduced by breast-feeding. Overall, however, there is no reduction in atopy apart from this specific circumstance. Although there are confounding variables which make study of the effect of breast-feeding on neurological development difficult, there is work that suggests that neurological development is enhanced in breast-fed infants. Infants who are breast-fed have a reduced risk of developing diabetes. There is no good evidence to show that breast-feeding reduces the incidence of infantile colic.

231:True 232:False 233:False 234:True 235:True

The testis are undescended in 3% of babies born at term and in 1% at the age of 12 months. Spontaneous descent is very rare after the first birthday. True undescended testis must be distinguished from retractile testis which can be 'milked' down into the scrotum. Impalpable testis are not necessarily absent and may be intra-abdominal. The incidence of undescended testis is much higher in preterm babies. 30% of cases are bilateral. There is an increased risk of infertility and of malignancy in children with undescended testis. In order to minimise these, orchidopexy should be carried out before the end of the second year. The incidence of testicular tumours in adults is 3 per 10,000. The risk in males with a history of undescended testis is 4—40 times greater. 60% of the tumours are seminomas, most of the remainder being teratomas.

Important associations of undescended testis:
• spinal muscular atrophy
• myotonic dystrophy
• x-linked icthyosis
• Kallmann's syndrome
• prune belly syndrome

236:True 237:True 238:False 239:True 240:True

Rectal bleeding should not be accepted as due to IBS and should always alert the physician to an organic cause. Loss of weight can occur but is usually of a few pounds only and associated with anorexia.

241:False 242:True 243:True 244:True 245:False

In a normal distribution, mean, median and mode are all of the same value. 99.7% of the population lie within 3 standard deviations of the mean. The standard deviation is the square root of the variance.

246:True 247:True 248:True 249:False 250:False

Suicide in alcoholics is especially prevalent during relapses after a period of abstinence. If episodes of aggression are directed towards themselves they are particularly at risk. The social and psychological isolation engendered by physical illness leaves patients at an immense risk. An urban environment is more associated with suicide than a rural one. The most vulnerable people are male, older age and single, but there has been an increase recently in the incidence in younger males.

251:False 252:True 253:True 254:True 255:False

Only insomnia, poor memory and anxiety are benefited, and in long-term studies (cross- over at 6 months) only insomnia and poor memory were improved.

256:True 257:True 258:True 259:True 260:True

Suicide is most common amongst elderly men, although rates amongst young men have been rising dramatically in recent years. Rates increase progressively through the married, never married, widowers and widows and the divorced. Suicide is increased amongst social classes I and V, individuals with a past history of suicide attempts, history of depression, alcohol abuse, drug abuse, schizophrenia or antisocial or borderline personality disorders. Feelings of hopeless-ness are an important predictor of immediate and long-term suicide risk. In most cases a warning is given before committing suicide with 2/3 expressing suicidal ideas to relatives and 1/3 expressing clear suicidal intent. 40% of suicide completers had consulted their GP in the previous week.

261:False 262:True 263:False 264:True 265:True

Rogers' technique of client-centred therapy is aimed at facilitating the client in achieving solutions to his own problems by his own efforts. It is non-judgemental, non-directive and non-interpretive. A principal aim is the acquisition of insight by the client.

266:True 267:True 268:True 269:False 270:True

Rice, maize and soya can be used as substitutes; all the others contain gluten.

271:True 272:True 273:False 274:False 275:True

In 1992 the *Haemophilus influenzae* B (HiB) vaccine was introduced. Since then *Haemophilus influenzae*, meningitis, epiglottitis and other serious infections with this organism have virtually disappeared from paediatric wards. In 1994, mass measles and rubella vaccination was administered to prevent the predicted epidemic of measles in school-children. The immunisation covered over 8 million children. Since then there have only been a few confirmed cases of measles in schoolchildren. Smallpox was declared to have been eradicated from the world in 1980 by the World Health Organization. The last naturally occurring case of smallpox was in Somalia in 1977. The last epidemic of smallpox in London was at the turn of the century. Influenza A viruses are antigenically labile due to changes in the surface antigen haemagglutinin (H) and neuramidase (N). Minor changes (so called antigenic drift) occur from season to season. Major changes (i.e. antigenic shift) occur due to acquisition of a new haemagglutinin. Influenza B may undergo minor changes (less frequently than influenza A) and does not undergo major changes.

276:False 277:False 278:True 279:True 280:True

Primitive reflexes, such as the grasp reflex and rooting reflex, are signs of a frontal lobe lesion. Other signs of frontal lobe lesion include emotional lability, intellectual impairment, personality change, urinary incontinence and mono- or hemiparesis. Damage to the left frontal region produces Broca's aphasia. Parietal lobe lesions produce a variety of signs. Damage to either parietal lobe will produce contralateral sensory loss or neglect (another term is sensory hemi-inattention). Constructional apraxia, agraphasthesia, a failure to recognise surroundings, limb apraxia and homonymous field defect are also signs. The homonymous defect affecting the parietal lobe alone will produce a homonymous quadrantanopia affecting the lower quadrant compared with an upper field defect which occurs with a temporal lobe lesion. Specific damage to the right parietal region causes a dressing apraxia, and a failure to recognise faces, as well as the above. Damage to the left parietal region can produce Gerstmann's syndrome, consisting of dyscalculia, dysgraphia and left to right disorientation. Although it is not scientific and should not be quoted in an exam, it is helpful to think of the parietal lobes as being responsible for position in space and in addition to this the right lobe is also concerned with the artistic sociable side, whereas the left is the more studious and mathematical side.

281:True 282:False 283:False 284:True 285:False

Sudden infant death is the unexpected and unexplained death of an infant (on post-mortem findings and on examination of the scene of death). The peak incidence is at 2—4 months of age with 95% of deaths occurring before 6 months of age. The incidence has been declining since 1989 when there were 1,337 deaths, to 442 deaths in 1993. The incidence started declining before the government's *Back to Sleep* campaign in 1991 which promoted sleep in the supine position, probably due to prior publicity of the need to put babies to sleep supine.
The major risk factors for sudden infant death syndrome (SIDS):
• parental smoking — antenatal and postnatal
• prone sleeping position
• male sex
• maternal age (younger)
• low birth weight
• prematurity
• febrile illness
• thermal stress (high temperature, over wrapping).

The use of apnoea monitors has not reduced the risk of SIDS. There is no proven association of SIDS with the type of mattress used.

286:True 287:False 288:True 289:False 290:False

Glaucoma, hypertension, diabetes, some haematological disorders and occasionally systemic inflammatory disorders are risk factors for retinal vein occlusion. The onset of symptoms is not abrupt (by comparison with retinal artery occlusion) and may occur overnight. Thus the patient wakes with blurred vision which may develop into blindness. Retinal haemorrhages are the characteristic feature of retinal vein occlusion. If it is a central vein occlusion they occur throughout the fundus. With a branch occlusion a wedge-shaped area of haemorrhage appears in the area the vein drains with the apex of the wedge pointing to the optic disc. Improvement of the vision of the affected eye may occur. There are no studies of the benefit of long-term aspirin for retinal vein occlusion.

291:True 292:False 293:False 294:True 295:False

A low serum B12 is associated with dietary deficiency (true vegans), and malabsorption due to pernicious anaemia, partial/total gastrectomy or Crohn's disease, ileal resection, blind loop syndrome or fish tapeworm.

296:True 297:False 298:True 299:True 300:True

This condition, which is almost (though not entirely) confined to females, is also strongly associated with the use of vaginal tampons and is believed to be caused by toxins produced by *Staphylococcus aureus*.

301:False 302:True 303:False 304:True 305:True

There is generally a latent period of 15—40 years between exposure to asbestos and disease. Following diagnosis, symptomatic treatment is all that can usefully be offered.

306:False 307:True 308:False 309:False 310:True

Microalbuminuria is the first manifestation of diabetic nephropathy, but it may not occur until the second to third decades after the diagnosis of diabetes. It is best assessed by examination of early morning urine specimens, as albumin excretion can vary diurnally. Albuminuria can be reduced by optimising glycaemic control and blood pressure; ACE inhibitor agents have been shown to be of particular benefit in the treatment of hypertension.

311:True 312:False 313:False 314:False 315:True

The use of mesalazine to maintain remission in ulcerative colitis is well established. More recently high doses of slow-release mesalazine have been shown to be effective in the treatment of active small bowel Crohn's disease. Generally 5-acetylsalicylic acid compounds are safe in pregnancy and do not produce impotence, although sulphasalazine causes oligospermia, a side-effect attributable to its sulphapyridine moiety. Acetylsalicylic acid foam enemas are now available as effective treatment for colitis of the rectosigmoid colon.

316:False 317:True 318:True 319:False 320:False

Polycystic kidney disease is associated with hepatic cysts (in about 70% of cases) and also pancreatic cysts, although failure of the respective organs is rare. Berry aneurysms in the cerebral circulation occur in 25% of patients. Large or infected kidneys may need to be removed prior to transplantation.

321:True 322:False 323:False 324:False 325:False

Epidemiological studies have shown that a diet high in animal fat and low in fruit and vegetable fibre predisposes to colon cancer. Familial adenomatous polyposis coli (FAPC) is an uncommon disorder, inherited in autosomal dominant manner and inevitably results in colon cancer. It accounts for approximately 1% of all cases. The FAPC gene is located on chromosome 5. In contrast, hereditary non-polyposis colorectal cancer (HNPCC) is relatively common accounting for up to 15% of cases of colon cancer. The familial colorectal cancer gene is linked to chromosome 2 and is also dominantly inherited. Faecal occult blood testing is a sensitive test for gastrointestinal blood loss but its sensitivity and specificity is too low for it to be of value in the detection of colon cancer.

326:True 327:False 328:False 329:False 330:False

A thorough knowledge of immunisation is required and you should refer to the current *Handbook of Immunisation.* Contraindications and indications to vaccination depend on the vaccine used and the medical condition of the child.

Immunocompromised individuals (e.g. congenital immune disorders, children on high dose corticosteroids or immunosuppressive therapy and children with malignancy or other tumours of the reticulo-endothelial system) should not receive live vaccines. Live polio vaccine should not be given to siblings of immunocompromised individuals due to the risk of viral transmission, instead killed (Salk) polio virus vaccine should be given. HIV positive individuals with or without symptoms can receive MMR and polio live vaccines. They should not receive BCG, yellow fever or oral typhoid vaccines.

DTP vaccination is contraindicated if, on previous exposure, there have been seizures within 3 days of vaccine, encephalitis or collapse and shock (all associated with pertussis component). Reactions to pertussis vaccination are reduced in studies using the acellular pertussis vaccines rather than cellular pertussis vaccines.

MMR, influenza and yellow fever vaccines produced in chick embryos are contraindicated in children with a history of having had an anaphylactic reaction to egg. The most recent *Handbook of Immunisation* suggests that MMR is probably safe even if the child has had an anaphylactic reaction to egg. Cases in which there is any concern should be immunised in hospital. The most common side-effects after MMR vaccination are fever and rash a week after vaccination. Parotid swelling occasionally occurs in the third week. The incidence of meningoencephalitis (rare, with complete recovery) has fallen since the change in the mumps vaccine component of MMR.

Live vaccines are ineffective up to 3—12 months after immunoglobulin infusions, they are also less effective if given within 3 weeks of a previous live vaccine.

Common side-effects of **BCG vaccination** include localised skin ulceration, sterile abscess at injection site and regional adenitis. BCG vaccine should only be given after testing for hypersensitivity to tuberculoprotein, except in newborn infants where testing is not necessary before vaccine is given.

Influenza vaccines are recommended only for children at high risk e.g. chronic respiratory disease (including asthma, bronchopulmonary dysplasia and cystic fibrosis), chronic heart disease, chronic renal disease, diabetes mellitus and other endocrine disorders.

Pneumococcal vaccine is indicated in those at increased risk of pneumococcal infection e.g. sickle cell disease, asplenic patients, immunocompromised children (including HIV). It has minimal effect if given before the age of 2 years.

331:False 332:True 333:False 334:False 335:False

The 3rd cranial nerve supplies the levator of the eyelid, the medial, superior, inferior recti and the inferior oblique muscles. Paralysis causes ptosis, a dilated pupil and paralysis of action of the above-named muscles. Abduction of the eye is intact because the lateral rectus responsible for this action is supplied by the 6th cranial nerve. Direct light reflex is lost as the efferent part of the reflex is via the 3rd cranial nerve.

336:False 337:True 338:False 339:True 340:True

Well circumscribed, painless, superficial reddened erosions occur on the penis, usually on the glans (circinate balanitis) but sometimes more extensively. Conjunctivitis is the more characteristic eye lesion, but anterior uveitis and (rarely) superficial keratitis may also occur. Subungual keratosis is usually associated with keratodermia blennorrhagica affecting the soles and sometimes the palms.

341:False 342:False 343:True 344:False 345:False

Infectious mononucleosis (IM) is most easily and cheaply diagnosed by use of the Monospot test for heterophile antibodies in the patient's serum. IM is almost always more severe in adolescents and adults than in children, possibly because the former are capable of a more exuberant immunological reaction to the foreign body. Aspirin and bed rest are the recommended treatment for most uncomplicated adolescent cases. IM spreads characteristically sporadically. The IM fever may rise to 40° C during the day and marked swings are unusual.

346:False 347:False 348:False 349:False 350:True

Thyroid cancer and hyperthyroidism rarely co-exist. Thyroid cancer is characteristically a 'cold nodule' on radioisotope scanning of the thyroid gland. The commonest cancer in the young patient is papillary carcinoma and the anaplastic tumours typically occur in the elderly. Follicular carcinomas particularly metastasise to bone and the papillary type carries a better prognosis than the follicular type.

351:True 352:True 353:False 354:True 355:True

Migrainous neuralgia is classically precipitated by alcohol, the attacks usually lasting 2—6 hours. There may be associated ptosis, ocular disturbance, corneal suffusion, increased lacrimation and nasal stuffiness on the same side and endophthalmus. The attacks are unilateral but may affect either side in different attacks.

356:False 357:True 358:True 359:True 360:True

Normal developmental milestones:

- **4–6 weeks**
  Smiles.
- **6 weeks**
  Prone —pelvis flat. Ventral suspension — head up to plane of body momentarily. Fixes and follows in the horizontal plane.
- **12–16 weeks**
  Prone supports on forearms. Fixes and follows in the horizontal and vertical plane.
- **20 weeks**
  Full head control. No head lag when pulled to sit. Reaches for objects and grabs them.
- **6 months**
  Prone weight bears on hands. Rolls prone to supine. Transfers hand to hand. Chews. Feeds with a biscuit.
- **7 months**
  Rolls supine to prone. Sits hands held forwards for support.
- **9 months**
  Finger thumb opposition. Sitting can lean forward and recover position. Waves bye-bye. Starting to stand with support from furniture.
- **1 year**
  Walking with one hand held. Uses two words with meaning. Mouthing stops.
- **13 months**
  Stands alone for a moment.
- **18 months**
  Goes up and down stairs holding rail. Can throw a ball without falling. Domestic mimicry. Feeds with spoon. Spontaneous scribble. Takes off socks and shoes. Can follow simple orders. Uses many words, jargon still present. Tower of 3—4 cubes. Dry in day.
- **2 years**
  Goes up and down stairs two feet per step. Kicks ball without falling. Washes and dries hands. Tower of 6—7 cubes. Puts on socks, pants and shoes. Imitates vertical stroke. Turns pages one at a time. Joins two words in sentences.

- **2.5 years**

  Jumps with both feet. Walks on tiptoes. Pencil held in hand not in fist. Knows sex and full name. Names one colour.

- **3 years**

  Upstairs one foot per step, downstairs two feet per step. Rides tricycle. Attends to toilet needs without help. Dresses and undresses if helped with buttons and shoes. Names two colours. Constantly asks questions. Copies a circle.

- **4 years**

  Up and downstairs one foot per step. Buttons clothes fully. Catches a ball. Copies a cross. Names three colours. Speech is grammatically correct and can give age. Eats with spoon and fork. Brushes teeth. Understands taking turns and sharing. Distinguishes past, present and future and right and left. Can hop for a few seconds on each foot.

- **5 years**

  Can skip and hop. Drawing skills are improved — draws square (4.5 years) and triangle (5.5 years), can write a few letters. Names four colours. Can give home address. Distinguishes morning from afternoon. Dresses and undresses alone. Chooses own friends. Understands needs for rules in games and play.

361:False 362:False 363:True 364:True 365:False

An undescended testis lies anywhere along the course of descent from the abdomen to the scrotum. It is usually accompanied by a congenital inguinal hernia. Most cases are recognised in infancy or childhood and should be corrected early, if possible by the age of 2 years. An undescended testis predisposes to malignancy. The affected testis may be small and fertility may be impaired but if the other testis is functioning normally, this prevents sterility. There is an increased risk of torsion.

366:False 367:True 368:True 369:False 370:True

Most studies indicate that a working class background predisposes to major depression. Unemployment, rather than continuous employment, is a major factor in the aetiology of depression.

371:True 372:True 373:False 374:True 375:True

Agitation and retardation both occur in a significant number of elderly depressives. When delusions are present, they usually have a depressive flavour (e.g. poverty or physical illness). A certain proportion have apparent cognitive deficits, which improve in parallel with the symptoms of depression: this is the commonest variety of 'pseudo-dementia'. Severe life events can precipitate depression in the elderly, but bereavement is less important as a cause of mental illness than in younger age groups.

376:False 377:True 378:False 379:True 380:False

A statistically significant association is usually at a level of $p < 0.01$— 0.001 (i.e. there is less than a one in a hundred chance of the association occurring by chance). The association is not proven.

381:True 382:True 383:True 384:True 385:False

General practitioner contracts state that the individual doctor is responsible for care at all times, even if this care is delegated to a deputising service or practice nurse. The GP is also responsible for all employed staff and also their family, if they answer the telephone. If a GP perceives the need for a drug and it is available on an NHS prescription it must be provided. A private prescription cannot be used even if the drug is cheaper to the patient privately. Of course if it is available 'over the counter' without a prescription the patient can be advised of this. The commonest reason for a complaint against a GP is failure to visit.

386:True 387:True 388:True 389:False 390:True

Spontaneous rib fractures may occur in the absence of trauma when there is an abnormality of the rib. This may be due to osteoporosis, primary lung tumour or metastatic disease. Tumours that spread to bone include breast, lung, thyroid, kidney and prostate. Trauma may obviously cause a rib fracture but coughing, especially in the elderly, may be sufficient to cause several fractures. A rib fracture may cause a pneumothorax but not vice versa.

391:False 392:True 393:True 394:False 395:False

Stroke management involves both medical and surgical measures. Aspirin and warfarin are used for primary prevention of embolic stroke for patients in atrial fibrillation. Aspirin is used when the risk is low, warfarin is given when the risk is high. Patients at low risk include those under 65 years of age with no family history, no structural heart disease, and no previous transient ischaemic attacks (TIA) or myocardial infarction. High risk patients include those aged 65+ who have had previous TIA or MI, and all patients aged 85+.

Management of stroke

Nursing input — turning and feeding
Dietary — IV fluids, NG tube, PEG tube, parenteral feeding
Physiotherapy — to encourage mobilisation
Occupational therapy and psychological support

A carotid bruit does not justify surgery. A Doppler study, angiography or MRI is required. MRI scans are not routinely used for stroke management. CT is the best investigation and is useful to distinguish infarction from haemorrhage.

396:True 397:False 398:True 399:True 400:False

Dark urine may occur due to:
• pigments (e.g. beetroot)
• drugs (e.g. rifampicin)
• haemoglobin and its metabolic products (e.g. bilirubin)
• porphyria (urine darkens on standing)
• intravascular haemolysis (e.g. malaria — hence the term 'black water fever').

Conjugated bilirubin is water soluble and appears in the urine but unconjugated urine is colourless. Gilbert's syndrome is a hereditary condition where there is a lack of the conjugating enzyme producing increased unconjugated bilirubin. Heavy proteinuria can cause the urine to be white and frothy.

401:True 402:True 403:False 404:True 405:True

Indications of a severe outcome include onset with brain-stem or cerebellar lesions, onset after the age of 40 and disease that is progressive from the onset.

406:True 407:False 408:False 409:True 410:True

It is usually present in all positions, whether lying down or not, and it is likely to become strangulated.

411:True 412:True 413:False 414:False 415:True

It is not a legal requirement to keep a copy of the script, merely good practice. The patient can obtain supplies from any pharmacy.

416:False 417:False 418:False 419:True 420:False

Bacterial vaginosis used to be known as non-specific vaginitis or *Gardnerella vaginalis,* but it is now thought not to be caused by a single organism. Instead a change in the vaginal milieu allows colonisation with a range of organisms including mycoplasmas, gardnerella and anaerobic bacteria. There is no inflammation of the bacterial wall (unlike in candidiasis and trichomoniasis) which explains the modern use of the term vaginosis rather than vaginitis. The common symptoms of bacterial vaginosis are vaginal discharge and an unpleasant odour (particularly after intercourse) but not pruritus. Metronidazole is the most commonly used antibiotic; intravaginal clindamycin is also effective. Ampicillin or amoxycillin have only 50% efficacy while quinalones, tetracycline and erythromycin are ineffective. Recurrent attacks are common, perhaps because therapy is directed towards eliminating organisms rather than re-establishing the normal vaginal flora.

421:True 422:False 423:False 424:True 425:False

Anorexia nervosa is defined by self-induced weight loss, abnormal attitudes to food and body weight and amenorrhoea in women or loss of libido in men. There are many endocrine changes e.g. raised cortisol and growth hormone, and decreased gonadotrophins. However, there is little evidence that it is a primary endocrinological disorder. Structural lesions are rarely discovered. Clinical features include lanugo, a type of downy hair found on the extremities. Induced vomiting and purging to reduce weight often result in hypokalaemia.

426:False 427:False 428:False 429:True 430:False

EEG test result	True diagnosis	
	Seizures	No seizures
Positive	30	10
Negative	20	90
Total	50	100

Sensitivity = 30/50 x 100 = 60%; Specificity = 90/100 x 100 = 90%

The sensitivity and specificity are independent of the disease prevalence in the population being tested. The low sensitivity of an EEG implies an unacceptably high false negative rate for a serious condition such as seizures. The positive predictive value is a test's ability to identify those persons who truly have the disease from among all those persons whose screening tests are positive. In this example the positive predictive value (75%) is the number of persons with disease who screen positive (30) divided by the total number of persons who screen positive (40).

Out of 1000 people screened, 50 will have the disease, a prevalence of 5%. The number of false positives will be 95.

EEG test results	True diagnosis		
	Seizures	No seizures	Total
Positive	30	95	125
Negative	20	855	875
Total	50	950	1000

431:True 432:True 433:False 434:True 435:False

Bereavement reactions are normal, but share features in common with depression such as misery, tearfulness, insomnia, poor concentration and anorexia. Other features of depression such as psychomotor retardation, delusions, suicidal thinking and generalised loss of self-esteem only rarely occur in bereavement. Physical symptoms are more commonly reported by the bereaved. Most typically, three stages of grieving can be distinguished: an initial phase of emotional numbness and unreality; secondly a mourning phase of variable length which may include experiences of the presence or voice of the deceased and searching behaviour; finally there is gradual acceptance and resolution.

436:True 437:True 438:True 439:False 440:False

Gynaecomastia occurs rarely with omeprazole and is more commonly seen with H_2- antagonist treatment. Severe headache is probably the most common reason for discontinuing omeprazole therapy. Bradycardia, occasionally due to atrioventricular block, and pancreatitis have not yet been reported with omeprazole but both are recognised side-effects of H_2-antagonist treatment.

441:False 442:True 443:False 444:False 445:True

An IUCD is an effective method for 5 days after coitus. The morning after pill is only effective for 3 days. There is no teratogenic risk to the fetus and it is not contraindicated when breast-feeding. Mastalgia is in fact a side effect in the non-pregnant woman. Because 50% of the female population is unaware of these methods they have failed to reduce unplanned pregnancies.

446:True 447:False 448:True 449:True 450:False

Glaucoma is three times more common in blacks than in whites. The most important diagnostic features are cupping of the optic disc and loss of peripheral vision; intraocular pressure measurements are variable and of limited value.

451:True 452:False 453:True 454:True 455:False

Osteoporosis is most commonly age-related and/or post-menopausal. Other causes include hypogonadism, thyrotoxicosis, steroid excess, immobility, myeloma, rheumatoid arthritis, phenytoin and heparin. Bone density is reduced to less than 2.5 standard deviation units below that of healthy young subjects. There are no biochemical markers that fall outside the normal range, although bone formation (indicated by serum osteocalcin, alkaline phosphatase and urinary procollagen peptides) must be lower than the rate of bone resorption (indicated by urinary hydroxyproline or pyridinium-collagen crosslinks). Treatment with biphosphonates, either cyclical etidronate or alendronate (continuously), have been shown to increase bone density and reduce vertebral fractures. Bone density is best measured by dual energy X-ray absorptiometry (DEXA) but the inaccuracy is such that significant changes can usually only be detected over 1—2 years.

456:True 457:True 458:False 459:False 460:False

Vesico-ureteric reflux often only presents as chronic renal failure in adult life; even at this stage ureteric reimplantation may be of benefit for symptomatic reflux. Evidence of urinary tract infection is only present in about 40% of cases.

461:True 462:True 463:True 464:False 465:False

Dermoid cysts may arise from epithelium along lines of embryological development. They may arise in the midline of the head and neck and may contain hair or other ectodermal structures.Sebaceous cysts are the most common skin cysts; they consist of stratified squamous lining epithelium filled with keratin. They are covered by normal epithelium and often have a punctum. They can occur anywhere but tend to occur where hair follicles are present. A thyroglossal cyst occurs in the midline. It is situated anywhere along the midline usually beneath the hyoid bone along the thyroglossal tract. This is the embryological tract of descent of the thyroid gland from the foramen caecum to its position in the neck. A diagnostic feature is that it moves on swallowing or protrusion of the tongue. A branchial cyst arises from the remnants of the second pharyngeal pouch. It is typically a painless soft swelling appearing deep to sternomastoid muscle and bulging forward at the anterior border. Cystic fibromas are lymphangiomas. They are present at birth and may be huge. They occur below the angle of the mandible on the side and not in the midline.

466:True 467:False 468:False 469:True 470:True

ACE inhibitors have been shown to reduce mortality post myocardial infarction (MI) in a number of studies. In the ISIS 4 trial captopril was used in all patients post MI and was shown to reduce overall mortality by 0.6—0.7% at 6 months. In the same trial nitrates were shown to be ineffective. The TRENT study found that nifedipine increased mortality post MI. Timolol was shown by the Norwegian Multicentre Group to reduce mortality by 7% over a 33 month period after MI. In the 4S study, simvastatin given to all patients with ischaemic heart disease and a cholesterol level > 5.4 reduced mortality by 30% at 6 years.

471:True 472:False 473:True 474:False 475:True

Conjunctivitis usually presents with redness of the conjunctiva, often affecting both eyes, and a sticky discharge of viral or bacterial origin. Episcleritis is a common complication of many systemic conditions and is not a threat to the sight, in contrast to scleritis which is a serious disorder and a threat to vision. Iritis presents with redness mostly round the cornea, pain, photophobia and corneal precipitates which may be visible. Keratitis is associated particularly with herpes virus infection and some vasculitides, whereas rheumatoid arthritis is associated with scleritis. The pain in acute glaucoma may be very intense and vomiting is common.

476:True 477:True 478:True 479:False 480:True

Hypercalcaemia may result from:
- increased intake/absorption (e.g. vitamin D excess, sarcoidosis, IV therapy)
- increased bone resorption (e.g. malignancy, hyperparathyroidism, thyrotoxicosis, immobilisation, renal failure)
- increased renal reabsorption (e.g. thiazide diuretic therapy)
- miscellaneous, (e.g. Addison's disease, acromegaly, vitamin D intoxication, tuberculosis, phaeochromocytoma)

481:False 482:False 483:False 484:True 485:False

Onset of schizophrenia, usually between 15 and 45 years of age, occurs on average five years earlier in males (median onset 28 years). One third of patients have a good or fair outcome and 10—20% a severe chronic illness. Deterioration in function usually plateaus after 3—5 years and florid symptoms often reduce with increasing age. Outcome is worse in developed countries, although incidence and symptomatology is similar worldwide. Increased prevalence within socio-economically deprived areas is due to downward 'social drift' after illness onset. High 'expressed emotion' in family members, particularly those with more than 35 hours per week contact with the patient, is highly predictive of relapse.

486:False 487:True 488:True 489:False 490:False

Retrograde amnesia is not a good prognostic factor. The duration of post-traumatic amnesia is more variable and is predictive of time to return to work, psychiatric disablement and personality change. Complete recall of the injury, particularly in an emotionally loaded setting, is predictive of neurotic disabilities. A personal or family history of mental disorder predicts later psychiatric incapacity. An increase in post-traumatic neurotic symptoms, intellectual and memory impairments and mortality is seen with increasing age. Compensation and litigation increase psychiatric sequelae, such symptoms being rare after injuries at sport or in the home where compensation is not payable. However settlement of compensation rarely leads to a significant resolution of psychiatric symptoms.

491:True 492:True 493:False 494:False 495:False

Specific contraindications to routine vaccination include:
* Febrile illness, intercurrent infections
* Hypersensitivity to egg protein contraindicates influenza vaccine; previous anaphylactic reaction to egg contraindicates measles/mumps/rubella, influenza and yellow fever vaccines
* Infantile eczema

No live vaccine should be administered in:
* Immunodeficiency or with immunosuppressive therapy, including high-dose corticosteroids
* Malignancy
* Pregnancy

496:False 497:True 498:True 499:False 500:False

The most common heart defects in Down's syndrome are atrioventricular canal defects (40% compared with 2—3% in the normal population), secundum atrial septal defect and patent ductus arteriosus. Aortic stenosis and coarctation of the aorta are rare. Nearly all Down's syndrome patients have some evidence of Alzheimer's disease by the time they are 40 years old. There is decreased prevalence of atherosclerosis in Down's syndrome, although the reasons for this are not clear. Deletion of chromosome 15q 11-13 is typical of the Prader-Willi syndrome. Trisomy 21 is the classical chromosomal abnormality in Down's syndrome.

APPROACH TO THE ORAL EXAMINATION COMPONENT

Revision of the oral component of the MRCGP has been necessary to accommodate the new modular format. In the past only 85% of the candidates taking the written papers carried on through to the orals. Changes within the oral have therefore been necessary firstly to accommodate the increased number of candidates taking this part of the examination and secondly to produce a marking system independent of the written papers.

The change to a modular system also has implications for you. You will need to decide on the optimum time to take this component and on how to prepare for it. A clear idea of the structure of the orals is essential for this, as is an understanding of what is being tested and how. All assessment procedures flow better when the rules of the game are clear!

What is being tested in the orals?

The oral exists to assess areas of competence not tested in other parts of the examination. MCQ-type questions test factual knowledge reliably and extensively; hard facts and figures are not a part of the oral assessment. Similarly, appraisal and knowledge of the medical literature is tested in the Current Awareness and Critical Appraisal components of the written papers and detailed description of trials and papers should not be retested. Neither should the type of problem set in the Modified Essay Question (Problem Solving) type component of the written papers be redebated. The oral has its own focus.

The aim is to assess the candidates' abilities to make decisions and to justify the conclusions they reach, in the face of critical challenge from the examiners. Situations will be set or clinical problems raised which the candidate is asked to critically think about and discuss.

It is important to understand this since demonstration of the decision making process to the examiner is an essential part of the oral assessment.

An approach that analyses options and can look at the advantages and disadvantages of the possible solution before a final conclusion is reached, will inevitably gain more credit. A straightforward response such as: 'In this situation, I would without hesitation do this,' may seem decisive but may be viewed as rigid or dogmatic. The reasoning process is being examined far more than the ultimate decision is being judged.

For example, take the situation of an unreasonable out of hours call from a mother requesting a visit for her 5-year-old son who has a sore throat. The examiner will not be awarding you marks for thinking 'This is the college examination and I must give the gold standard answer that: I would visit without hesitation in case she was worried he had meningitis!' The ultimate decision 'to go or not to go' is not as highly weighted in the marking scheme as the candidate's ability to look at the options available and to weigh up the pros and cons of each one before justifying a decision. Why is she asking for the visit? What are your on call arrangements? How well do you know her? How experienced are you as a GP? These are only some of the factors affecting the response. Decision making is the process being tested with justification of any conclusions reached. There may be no black and white (i.e. right or wrong answer): after all a lot of our working life operates in the grey area!

What is the structure of the new orals?

There are two 20-minute oral examinations, each with two examiners. These occur consecutively with an approximate 10-minute break in between for changing tables. The practice experience questionnaire, used in the past, is no longer required.

In each oral, the candidate answers four or five questions. Both oral sessions are structured in the same way and both focus on testing decision making skills in different situations. The topics to be covered are planned in advance by the four examiners. This ensures that the oral covers a fair range of general practice subjects and that there is no overlap between the issues covered.

When meeting to plan the oral, examiners have no knowledge of the candidate's marks if other modules of the examination have already been taken. They cannot link their questions to the candidate's previous performance in any way. Thus the candidate will gain four individual and independent marks during the course of the orals. Marks can differ significantly between the two orals. Therefore during the break use the time to recover. Relax and put the previous experience behind you. Approach your second oral in a positive frame of mind.

After each pair of orals, the four examiners will meet to assess the candidate's marks and reach a final pass/fail decision.

What range of questions is asked?

The examiners plan the orals together to cover as wide a range of topics as possible. The aim is to create a fair examination by testing decision making in as many different contexts as possible and avoiding repetition.

To do this a structure has been designed.

Three principal areas of assessment of the candidate's competence have been identified for testing in the orals:

- ***Communication.*** This encompasses verbal and non-verbal communication techniques, skills for effective information transfer and principles of communication and consultation models
- ***Professional values.*** This covers general moral and ethical issues, patient autonomy, medico-legal issues, flexibility and tolerance, implications of styles of practice, roles of health professionals and cultural and social factors
- ***Personal and professional growth.*** This focuses on the candidate's personal approach to continuing professional development, self-appraisal and evaluation, stress awareness and management, burnout and change management.

In order to focus and achieve a wide sample of questions these three competencies are tested in four areas or contexts relevant to general practice:

- The care of the patient specifically
- Working with colleagues (Primary health care team and others beyond)
- Society as a whole
- Taking personal responsibility (for care, decisions, outcomes).

Questions testing each competency should focus on one of these four areas. Candidates should be aware of this structure as examiners may indicate, when phrasing a question, in which area they plan to mark.

Example

Take the topic of diabetes, which can clearly be used to focus questions in many different ways.

The examiner may say:
'I would like to ask you a question looking at your communication skills.
How would you explain to an 80-year-old patient that the nurse has found sugar in her urine and she probably has diabetes?'
In answering this, candidates should focus on how they would use their **communication skills** with an individual **patient** in this age group.

Alternatively the examiner may say:
'I would like to ask you a question that focuses on your own personal development. You are concerned that you are becoming deskilled in managing diabetes since your partner took on responsibility for managing the practice diabetic clinic. What could you do about this?'
This question is entirely focused on the candidate's **individual personal development** and the candidate should answer this at a **personal level**.

Alternatively the examiner may ask:
'I would like you to consider a situation that affects our professional values as a practice team. It is clear from your PACT figures that prescribing costs for blood glucose testing stix have significantly increased over the past six months. You have a new nurse running the diabetic clinic who is not following the practice protocol. What issues does this raise for you as a team?'
The approach to answering this question should be entirely different, concentrating on problems of differing **attitudes and values** which need addressing in managing a disease such as diabetes within a **multi-professional team**.

From the candidate's point of view it is clearly important to listen carefully to the question, to clarify it if uncertain what is being asked and to keep to the area in which the question has been focused. If it is an area in which you know very little and are performing poorly, you should say so and enable the examiners to move on to the next question where performance may be significantly better.

How is the oral marked?

Both examiners mark each question independently and at the end of the oral reach a final overall grade, exclusive of each other. Thus, over the two orals, four grades are obtained which are entirely independent of performance in any of the other modules.

The candidate's response is graded against a written scale. There are nine potential categories ranging from 'outstanding' through to 'dangerous.' The average passing grade is 'satisfactory.' To achieve this grade, the candidate must be:

'A candidate characterised by a reassuring solidness rather than impressiveness. Able to justify only some approaches well, but most appear sensible. Adequate, not good, decision making skills.'

It follows that a spread of grading is achieved with the mean around the satisfactory level. 'Outstanding' and 'dangerous' grades are used only in extremely rare circumstances.

It is important for both examiners and candidates to recognise that each question must be structured in a way that will test a range of responses. It must enable the examiner to make a decision at the pass/fail level but at the same time have the capacity to test a candidate at merit level.

Recognition of this from the candidate's point of view is important for two reasons.

Firstly, as each question proceeds, it will get progressively more difficult and if the candidates are being examined well they will almost inevitably find there is a point beyond which they cannot deliver information. Thus they have reached their own personal level on the calibration scale and they will have no idea of this, beyond an uncomfortable feeling that they have not been able to stretch their answer to match the examiner's probing.

This cannot be avoided. It is an examination. Thus even excellent candidates when stretched to the limit may feel they are performing poorly. It is crucial to come to terms with this feeling and not panic! It is intrinsic to the examination process.

Secondly it may be equally difficult for a candidate at the pass/fail level to gauge his/her performance in the face of lack of any feedback from the examiners. The key is to take every question as it comes, approach each new one afresh and recognise that discomfort may be an inevitable part of the process.

The examiners are trained to make every effort to make the candidate feel welcome and at ease, the discomfort and uncertainty of an examination process cannot be avoided.

When should I take the oral?

As the modular form of the examination has not run before, there is no data on which to base this answer at the time of writing. However, although the oral does not specifically test factual knowledge and evidence-based practice, it can be seen that the process of decision making and justification cannot take place in a vacuum. A background of knowledge, awareness of the literature and experience of practice are required for you to justify your approach to decision making as a GP. Inevitably therefore the oral will be best approached towards the end of vocational training and with sufficient experience.

Helpful hints on approaching the orals

It is important to keep up to date. You do need to prepare for the oral. Working in pairs or as small groups can be stimulating. Questions can easily be devised and working out ways of increasing the difficulty of each question can be very educational.

The examiners are practising general practitioners from all over the United Kingdom who have been selected and trained. Full understanding of all aspects of British general practice is crucial. The oral will not focus on the candidate's area of practice but will expect a broad understanding of general practice: for example an inner city GP could be asked about the problems of rural practice.

What happens on the day?

It is important to treat the event as one would any professional interview: dress smartly and allow plenty of time for travel. Candidates are briefed by the examiner marshal before the orals start. It is not a good idea to arrive at the very last minute.

All the examiners have been selected through an assessment procedure. The successful ones are then trained before they start examining. Candidates are not allocated to examiners from their own region of practice and should, for obvious reasons, not be examined by anyone they know personally. As the number of MRCGP examinations throughout the UK expands, the situation occasionally arises where the candidate may have seen the examiner before. If the candidate recognises the examiners and would prefer not to be examined by them, a clear statement should be made immediately so that substitution can be arranged.

Observers may be present at the examination. Visitors from other medical faculties or professions attend to share and develop ideas for their own examination procedures. General practitioners interested in becoming examiners themselves observe for two days, before attending for the selection process, and experienced examiners may also observe for training purposes. The candidate should ignore any observer, as they are not contributing to the marking of the oral at all, only to the assessment of the examiners.

In addition, a candidate may occasionally be made aware that a video camera is recording the oral, for examiner training purposes. Again, candidates are reassured that only the examiners appear on the screen and the tape is used entirely for feedback to the examiners concerned and for teaching purposes within the panel.

An example of a question sequence in an oral:

Question	Topic	Area of competence			Context			
		Communication	Professional values	Personal & professional growth	Care of patients	Working with colleagues	Society	Personal responsibility
1	Minor illness		✓				✓	
2	Asthma	✓			✓			
3	Re-accreditation			✓				✓
4	Euthanasia		✓		✓			
5	Alcoholic partner	✓				✓		

Typical questions

Topic 1 — Minor illness

It could be said that in modern society, people are becoming de-skilled at handling minor illness. Why do you think that might be and what would you do about it?

As outlined in the grid on the previous page, this question is looking at our **professional values** as doctors in **society** and the candidate's decision making process in designing strategies to tackle this problem.

The answer should focus on the reasons for the public's loss of confidence in handling minor illness, which of the factors are most relevant to the GP's professional practice and working values and how the problem could be tackled. The better candidate will also be able to reflect on the use of the term 'minor illness' and how decisions could be reached to redefine the term.

Topic 2 — Asthma

You decide that a 3-year-old child, whom you have seen on several occasions with a dry cough, has asthma. How would you use your communication skills to explain the diagnosis to her mother?

This question is looking at the candidate's **consultation skills** and how decisions are reached in modifying them to explain the diagnosis in **the care of the patient**.

The answer should focus on eliciting the mother's understanding of the disease first before deciding what terms to use to explain the diagnosis at her level of understanding. The examiner might ask for the exact words the candidate would use and how he decided this. The question could extend for better candidates into the relevance of consultation models to this problem, which ones they might use and why.

Topic 3 — Re-accreditation

As you personally proceed with a career as a GP, how do you envisage future re-accreditation processes will develop and affect you as an individual?

This question is now in the area of ***personal*** responsibility for future **professional growth** through CME and re-accreditation.

Candidates would be expected to explore how decisions might be reached on a re-accreditation programme and how this would fit with their own wants, needs and learning styles with reference to personal decisions to be made in pursuing CME.

Topic 4 — Euthanasia

An 89-year-old patient of yours, bed-ridden with severe arthritis, asks you to explain to her honestly how many of the temazepam and phenobarbitone tablets stored in her cupboard she would need to take a fatal dose. What issues would this raise for you and how would you decide what to tell her?

This question is focused on ***professional values*** in ***the care of a patient***.

This question raises ethical issues relating to the legality of euthanasia balanced against truth telling and patient autonomy. Discussion of these would be relevant to the decision on how to respond professionally to this request. The examiner might expand the scenario by then suggesting that the patient was subsequently found dead in bed and the relatives are firmly against any thought of a post-mortem at her age. Further discussion of how to decide whether to inform the coroner or not and the ethical implications of the available options would be required.

Topic 5 — Alcoholic partner

Your health visitor asks to see you confidentially and reveals that several mothers have complained to her that your partner has alcohol on his breath even on morning visits. How would you respond to this?

This question deals with the competence area of ***professional values*** within the context of ***working with colleagues.***

Candidates should discuss the options open to them in dealing with this problem and the advantages and disadvantages of the various approaches with their inherent ethical issues. Awareness of the correct procedures for maintaining confidentiality while at the same time supporting the work interests of your colleague should form the focus of the discussion.

For further information on Ethical Problem Solving please turn to page 226.

APPROACH TO THE ASSESSMENT OF
CONSULTING SKILLS COMPONENT — VIDEO

In the past, the MRCGP examination has been criticised because there has been no assessment of clinical skills. The Royal College of General Practitioners has responded to this, and two approaches have now been developed –– the video component and the simulated surgery.

The video recording is the normal method of assessing consulting skills for the MRCGP. Candidates have to submit a video-recording of a sample of their recent consultations and this is accompanied by a completed workbook.

Preparing the video recording

Fifteen consultations need to be submitted, each lasting not longer than 15 minutes. All consultations must be conducted in English. At least two consultations must be with children under 10 years of age and at least two consultations must involve chronic disease in adult patients.

Valid consent must be given by patients for their consultation to be video-recorded and the appropriate consent forms must accompany the video and workbook. Detailed arrangement for consent and ethical guidelines are available in the publication *Assessment of Consulting Skills Workbook and Instructions* which is available to all applicants and is obtained through the RCGP Examinations Department. These ethical considerations also relate to the avoidance of physical examination of an intimate or sensitive nature and these must be conducted off camera. If these ethical guidelines and consent requirements are not adhered to, the video-recording will be returned and deemed to be void.

The recordings have to be of sufficiently good sound and picture quality and if they do not achieve this standard they will be rejected. Again, detailed requirements for the choice of camera, sound recording equipment, camera positioning and lighting are given in the *Workbook and Instructions*.

The Workbook

This contains the following sections:

- The competencies to be demonstrated. This sets out the competencies that the candidate is asked to demonstrate in the recorded consultations.
- Detailed instructions for recording consultations. This gives some practical advice about who should be recorded and how the recording should be made.
- Video tape log. This acts as an index to the tape, to help the examiners locate particular points in the recording.
- Consultation assessment forms. These are for the candidate's brief assessment of all recorded consultations.
- Detailed evaluation forms. These are for the detailed evaluation of five consultations that the candidate selects for particular consideration by the examiners.
- Ethical principles. These are the extracts from the RCGP's ethical guidelines on the recording of consultations.

How to approach the video component

After reading the ethical and practical considerations it is first of all important for the candidate to understand how the examiners approach assessment, so that the candidate has the best chance of succeeding. Consulting skills are a major element of professional competence for all general practitioners. Competence has three attributes that determine the way it is assessed.

- Competence is pre-defined. Candidates are given precise details about what the examiners are looking for. This is discussed later.
- Competence is about outcomes not behaviours. There are many ways in which a doctor can arrive at the successful completion of a consultation. The examiners do not make the assumption that there is only one acceptable way of achieving this outcome, since this is highly dependent on the individual style of the doctor being assessed.
- Competence is either present or absent. The examiners are judging whether or not the candidate has demonstrated competence in a particular situation. There is no measure of how well the candidate performs these specific competences.

The performance criteria

Specific performance criteria (PC) have been developed, which candidates will either meet or fail to meet during the consultation. Assessment is achieved by collecting evidence and making judgements on whether or not these performance criteria have been met. It should be possible for the candidate, another doctor, or an examiner to watch a recorded consultation and decide whether or not the particular performance criteria were achieved. Some performance criteria are proceeded by (P)—these are the criteria the examiners feel to be essential for a pass in consulting skills. Other performance criteria are proceeded by (M)—these are the criteria the examiners feel must be demonstrated for a pass with merit in consulting skills. The performance criteria are as follows, and are reproduced with the kind permission of the RCGP Examinations Department.

■ Discover the reason for a patient's attendance

a. ELICIT THE PATIENT'S ACCOUNT OF THE SYMPTOM(S) WHICH MADE HIM/HER TURN TO THE DOCTOR

(P)   PC: *the doctor encourages the patient's contribution at appropriate points in the consultation*

(P)   PC: *the doctor responds to cues*

b. OBTAIN RELEVANT ITEMS OF SOCIAL AND OCCUPATIONAL CIRCUMSTANCES

(P)   PC: *the doctor elicits appropriate details to place the complaint(s) in a social and psychological context*

c. EXPLORE THE PATIENT'S HEALTH UNDERSTANDING

(M)   PC: *the doctor takes the patient's health understanding into account*

d. ENQUIRE ABOUT CONTINUING PROBLEMS

   PC: *the doctor obtains enough information to assess whether a continuing complaint represents an issue that must be addressed in this consultation*

■ Define the clinical problem(s)

a. OBTAIN ADDITIONAL INFORMATION ABOUT SYMPTOMS AND DETAILS OF MEDICAL HISTORY

(P) PC: *the doctor obtains sufficient information for no serious condition to be missed*

    PC: *the doctor shows evidence of generating and testing hypotheses*

b. ASSESS THE CONDITION OF THE PATIENT BY APPROPRIATE PHYSICAL OR MENTAL EXAMINATION

(P) PC: *the doctor chooses an examination that is likely to confirm or disprove hypotheses which could reasonably have been formed OR to address a patient's concern*

c. MAKE A WORKING DIAGNOSIS

(P) PC: *the doctor appears to make a clinically appropriate working diagnosis*

■ Explain the problem(s) to the patient

a. SHARE THE FINDINGS WITH THE PATIENT

(P) PC: *the doctor explains the diagnosis, management and effects of treatment*

b. TAILOR THE EXPLANATION TO THE PATIENT

(P) PC: *the doctor explains in language appropriate to the patient*

(M) PC: *the doctor's explanation takes account of some or all of the patient's elicited beliefs*

c. ENSURE THAT THE EXPLANATION IS UNDERSTOOD AND ACCEPTED BY THE PATIENT

(M) PC: *the doctor seeks to confirm the patient's understanding*

Approach to the Assessment of Consulting Skills Component—Video

■ **Address the patient's problems**

a. ASSESS THE SEVERITY OF THE PATIENT'S PROBLEMS

(P) PC: *the doctor differentiates between problems of different degrees of severity and manages each appropriately*

b. CHOOSE AN APPROPRIATE FORM OF MANAGEMENT

(P) PC: *the doctor's management plan is appropriate for the working diagnosis, reflecting a good understanding of modern accepted medical practice*

c. INVOLVE THE PATIENT IN THE MANAGEMENT PLAN TO THE APPROPRIATE EXTENT

(P) PC: *the doctor shares management options with the patient*

■ **Make effective use of the consultation**

a. MAKE EFFICIENT USE OF RESOURCES

PC: *the doctor makes sensible use of available time and suggests further consultation as appropriate*

PC: *the doctor makes appropriate use of other health professionals through investigations, referrals, etc*

(P) PC: *the doctor's prescribing behaviour is appropriate*

b. ESTABLISH A RELATIONSHIP WITH THE PATIENT

(P) PC: *the patient and doctor appear to have established a rapport*

c. GIVE OPPORTUNISTIC HEALTH PROMOTION ADVICE

(P) PC: *the doctor deals appropriately with at-risk factors within the consultation*

Preparing the video-recording and workbook for submission

Candidates are required to gather evidence of their competence, and the chosen method for this involves the making of video-recordings of actual patients who consult the doctor in the course of the normal surgery, in the doctor's normal place of work. In addition a workbook is completed which involves reflecting on a selection of consultations, and committing these reflections to paper.

Candidates are allowed to choose which consultations they wish to present to the examiners so that they can show what they are capable of achieving if the consultation goes to plan. Allowing the candidate such a choice is to the candidate's advantage — a true impression of the candidate's consulting skills would require a large number of consultations to be viewed and this is obviously not feasible. The candidate is able to develop a 'mental picture' of what the performance criteria mean, and is able to show a trainer (or other mentor) their work for confirmation that they have demonstrated competence. It is wholly unacceptable for the workbook to be completed by someone other than the candidate, but the candidate can be guided on how to produce the evidence of competence.

It is worthwhile initially to read a text that gives a good overall summary of the consultation process and that highlights the skills required for the doctor in the consultations. Two particularly useful books are *The Doctors Communication Handbook* by Peter Tate published by Radcliffe Medical Press and *The Inner Consultation* by Roger Neighbour published by Petroc Press. After reading through these texts it should be clear what the various performance criteria mean and it should be possible to identify these performance criteria on a review of a particular consultation. The assistance of an experienced trainer or mentor is invaluable in helping the candidate to develop this self-assessment and reflection on their performance.

An example of a consultation and the highlighted performance criteria

Doctor   Hello Ian — what can I do for you today?

Patient   Well doctor — it's these pains in my stomach.

Doctor   Mmmm, please go on. (*Encourage patient's contribution.*)

Patient   Well — for the last three weeks I've had this pain in the centre of my stomach. It comes and goes. It is worse first thing in the morning- that's also when I get some diarrhoea.

Doctor   Can I ask you a few more questions? [There is then a symptomatic enquiry, concentrating on the nature, frequency, relieving and exacerbating factors of the pain, also identical features about the diarrhoea. Enquiry is also made about having passed any blood or slime and whether the man feels well and his weight has been steady]. (*Encourage patient's contribution and obtain enough information for no serious cause to be missed.*)

     I wonder if you have had any thoughts about these problems? (*Doctor takes the patient's health understanding into account.*)

Patient   I did read something about change in my bowels and indigestion in the newspaper and it said that I should see the doctor. I did wonder whether in fact it could be due to cancer or not.

Doctor   I see. Can I ask you a few more questions? I am not quite sure what job you do and whether there are any stresses or worries in your life at the moment. (*The doctor elicits appropriate details to place the complaint in a social and psychological context.*)

Patient   Well, I have had some worries at work with the recent merger. I am an accountant for the firm and the job is under threat of redundancy. My wife has just decided to give up work and she is now three months pregnant.

Doctor   I see you look rather worried about that. (*The doctor responds to cues.*)

Patient   I am worried in case we can't manage financially. There is a mortgage to pay and the car loan — we both had such good jobs.

Doctor	May I examine your abdomen now please? [The doctor examines the patient's abdomen.] (*The doctor chooses an examination that is likely to confirm or disprove hypotheses that have reasonably been formed or to address the patient's concern.*)
	I have now examined you and I am pleased to say that I could find no abnormality. Your story sounds like a condition called Irritable Bowel Syndrome. When you are under stress the body produces extra adrenaline which stimulates the stomach and the bowels to cause the abdominal pain and the diarrhoea. (*The doctor appears to make a clinically appropriate working diagnosis. The doctor explains in language appropriate to the patient.*)
	I do not think it is cancer because there is no blood or slime in the motion, and your weight is steady and I could not find an abnormality. (*The doctor's explanation takes account of some or all of the patient's elicited beliefs.*) How do you feel about that? (*The doctor seeks to confirm the patient's understanding.*)
Patient	Yes, I agree, it does sound like Irritable Bowel Syndrome.
Doctor	There are several options. If you are not too troubled and worried we could just leave it to see if it settles. I could offer you some tablets to stop the spasm. If you do feel concerned still I could arrange for some further investigations. (*The doctor shares management options with the patient, the doctor's prescribing behaviour is appropriate, the doctor's management plan is appropriate for the working diagnosis, reflecting a good understanding of modern accepted medical practice.*)
Patient	Well, I would rather have some tablets to relieve the pain.
Doctor	I will give you a prescription for some mebeverine. (*The doctor's prescribing behaviour is appropriate.*)
Patient	Thank you doctor, I will come back if there are any problems. (*The patient and doctor appear to have established a rapport.*)

Completing the video tape log

The function of the log is to allow the examiners to see at a glance the contents of the tape and to find parts that they wish to watch to assess the candidate's performance. For example, if the candidate states that he feels that he has demonstrated that he has shared management options with the patient, the examiner will seek this area out on the video-recording to confirm that what the candidate states he has done is actually present. Exact details on how the video tape log must be completed is found in the RCGP *Workbook and Instructions to Candidates.*

Consultation assessment

For every consultation recorded, a consultation assessment form must be completed. Each page is headed with a reference number, and this must correspond to the number used in the video-tape log and on the patient's consent form.

This consultation assessment provides an opportunity to put each consultation into its proper context. As the recording is reviewed it is helpful to try to put yourself into the position of someone watching the consultation for the first time and who has no prior knowledge about the patient or the circumstances of the consultation. For example, the patient may be the local vicar and the various comments about religion may be quite normal, rather than religious paranoid ideas! An example of a completed consultation assessment form is shown on the next page.

At the foot of each page in the workbook is a table which should be completed by the candidate to show which performance competencies the candidate feels have been demonstrated in the particular consultation.

CONSULTATION ASSESSMENT FORM

Ian

Age of patient: **32 years**   Sex of patient (M/F): **M**   Do you know the patient? **Yes**

Actual length of consultation (minutes): **11**   Booked length of consultation (minutes): **10**   New problem or follow-up? **New**

Presenting complaint(s):   **Abdominal pain and diarrhoea**

Relevant background information: **Never seen before**
(*e.g. previous knowledge of or consultation with this patient*)

Working diagnosis: **Irritable Bowel Syndrome**

Outcomes of the consultation: **Given prescription**
(*e.g. referral, no action, certificate, review*)

Prescription: **Given prescription for mebeverine**
(*provide full details of any* **135 mg t.d.s.**
prescription given or test ordered, with justification)

Any further points of clarification: **None**

encourage pt's contribution	cues	social/ psych context	obtain enough info	appropriate examination	appropriate diagnosis	diagnosis etc. explained	appropriate language	appropriate management	options shared	appropriate prescribing	rapport
√	√	√	√	√	√	√	√	√	√	√	√

Detailed evaluation

Candidates are required to carry out a detailed evaluation of five consultations and in the video tape log the consultations that have been chosen to be analysed are noted. The examiners may assess the candidate's competence on the basis of any part of the recording, but they will often particularly concentrate on this section. The recording of the consultation should be reviewed and after each minute of elapsed time the tape should be stopped and on the proforma there should be a description of any significant remarks, observations, thoughts, explanations or decisions. Also, a note should be made of any competence demonstrated in that minute. The examiners are interested in the candidate's own perceptions of what is happening and why, as the consultation unfolds minute by minute. It is more important to provide analysis and interpretation of the events than a mere factual account. An example of a completed evaluation form is shown on the next page.

Helpful hints in approaching the recording and the completion of the workbook

- Do not panic!
- Try to understand and be able to identify the key stages of the consultation process, linking this into the performance criteria that are required.
- Have a trial run first. Sit down with a trainer or mentor and work through a video-recording and begin to identify the performance criteria so as to be able to assess competence. Particularly, note any constructive comments made by the mentor or trainer.
- Finally, enjoy it!

DETAILED EVALUATION PROFORMA

Time in minutes	Observation	Competence demonstrated
0–1	Establish why Ian came today – abdominal pain, encourage to give own story	encourage patient's contribution
1–3	Further questions to establish working hypothesis and to exclude serious causes. Try to encourage Ian by minimal prompts	encourage patient's contribution
3–4	I tried to establish if Ian has any ideas or concerns about the abdominal pains. Ian wonders if it could be cancer	cues
4–6	Ask about work and home situation since may be precipitating factor for the pain	social/psych context
6–7	Ian identifies that he is under stress at work and at home. I pick up on Ian's anxiety – wife is due to stop working and possible financial difficulties	obtain enough info
7–9	Examine abdomen (out of camera shot) but no PR performed. No abnormality found	appropriate examination
9–10	I make a working diagnosis of Irritable Bowel Syndrome. Explanation of IBS linking symptoms to stress. Try to use simple language	diagnosis etc explained
10–11	Feedback negative features of cancer to Ian	diagnosis etc explained
11–12	Check Ian's understanding and acceptance of explanation – look for verbal and non-verbal signs	appropriate language
12–14	Explanation of management options, allowing Ian to choose his preferred options. Gave script for mebeverine 375mg 1t.d.s. before meals, 30 given	appropriate management plan
14–15	Ian leaves, looks relieved and obvious good rapport between us. Ian states will return if problems not settled or if worried	rapport

APPROACH TO ASSESSMENT OF CONSULTING SKILLS COMPONENT – SIMULATED SURGERY

Certain candidates will be unable to obtain a video-recording of the consultation, for example, if their normal consultations are performed in a language other than English or if there are any major moral or religious objections to video-recordings. In such exceptional circumstances these candidates can request, through the RCGP Examinations Department, that their consulting skills be assessed by taking part in a simulated surgery.

As the name implies, a simulation of a typical general practice surgery is given to candidates to assess their clinical competence. Candidates sit in a consulting room as if they were conducting an ordinary surgery and are visited in turn by eight or nine standardised patients, who are volunteer role players or actors. The scenarios acted out are based on case histories, taken from real life, and written by general practitioners.

In this way, every candidate is offered the same experience and each is assessed according to a marking schedule that has been devised specifically for each case. An observer is responsible for filling in an appropriate marking schedule and a mark is given as to whether the performance criteria have been appropriately achieved. Evaluation of this approach has shown simulated surgery to be a valid and reliable assessment tool.

The main skills assessed during a simulated surgery:

- Interview and history taking – the candidate takes a full focused history.
- Doctor–patient interaction – the candidate shows sensitivity towards the patient, is aware of, and facilitates a free expression of the patient's ideas and concerns, and offers a clear explanation to the patient.
- Physical examination – the candidate examines the patient appropriately, efficiently, and with courtesy and consideration.
- Patient management – the candidate negotiates a management with the patient, involves them in decisions, offers options, practises safe management, and uses resources and information appropriately.
- Anticipatory care – the candidate considers preventative care and anticipates the implication of his advice for the patient and for others.
- Ethical and moral issues – the candidate considers ethical issues in his practice, particularly patient confidentiality, and is able to offer reasons for his actions.

The simulated surgery is costly in terms of resources, role-players and markers. Currently it is in a process of evolution and in the next few years the exact format may change but all candidates wishing to take this component will be adequately informed of the intended changes **before** taking the simulated surgery.

PASSING THE MRCGP: A REGISTRAR'S VIEW

Written by Richard Bircher, a recent exam candidate.

Some of us see the MRCGP exam as a hurdle to jump to set us on course for a more fulfilled professional career and a better class of partnership. For me revision felt akin to an assault course, on a steep incline, in driving rain. I had two children under the age of two at home and foolishly ended my GP training scheme with a post in Obstetrics and Gynaecology with the obligatory 1:4 rota. Any revision had to be precise, effective and fitted around baby bath times and disturbed nights.

I admit, on the day of the exam, there was plenty I did not know but, to be honest, nothing surprised me in the written papers, video or viva. I was surprised to find I managed to predict half of the written paper and viva questions. At no point was I lost, running short of time or tongue tied and I felt more prepared for this exam than any others since the beginning of medical school. In offering advice on how to revise for the MRCGP I feel my best contribution is to explain how I personally prepared myself.

I started revising early, about 3 months before the written papers and averaged about 4–5 hours work a week. Most importantly, initially, I spent a good while looking at the task ahead and picked out the skills and information I had to assimilate. The Royal College makes this easy by sending the exam handbook to all candidates which lists the learning objectives for each part of the exam. I complemented their lists by looking through past papers and chatting to previous candidates. For me the necessary skills fell into three broad areas: attitudes, factual information and exam technique.

Any 'good' candidate should have a general awareness of the 'right' attitudes for the exam but I found it incredibly helpful to make these explicit at the outset. I made a list and tried to remain conscious of its content when reading any journal or book. It looked as follows.

Right attitudes for the exam

- Ability to think laterally
- Ability to realise long and short term effects of actions
- Ability to weigh up pros and cons of actions
- Ability critically to incorporate research and information into clinical work
- Ability to appreciate the wider aspects of general practice
- Self-awareness
- Sharing with patients
- Teamwork and management

What was intriguing about using this list was the way it directed my reading. For example, on the subject of sore throats, rather than limiting my study to the pros and cons of antibiotics I was led into looking at the long term consequences of my decisions in a sore throat consultation, their impact on the whole primary care team, issues of resource allocation, the stress of seeing 'inappropriate' self-limiting ailments, Nurse Practitioner schemes and dealing with demanding patients. At first glance some of these issues do not sit comfortably with the subject of sore throats but they were raised several times during the exam and probably scored me valuable points.

When planning my reading I found the greatest problem was one of inertia. Because general practice is such an enormous subject (some would argue one without boundaries) any reading has to be extensive. I cracked the problem by beginning with a brain storm of hot topics. I was lucky to be sitting the exam after my registrar year and was aware of many of the current controversies and dilemmas. It took one evening with a fellow registrar and a pile of copies of the *BJGP*, *Pulse* and the *BMJ* to produce a list of over 200 subjects. My trainer provided a few others. I allowed myself to add to this list constantly as I came across new areas of study or to remove items as it became apparent they were less useful. Some notable subjects were recent government papers, needs assessment and planning, the management of change, rationing and personal development. I purposely avoided an extensive list of diseases.

I read 'into' a subject by pulling out the paper which had brought it to my attention as a 'hot topic' or by looking at the *BMJ*, *BJGP* or *Lancet* indexes. I rarely read any paper in its entirety unless it was very influential and was crying out to be included in the exam, but rather limited myself to the initial summary, the introduction and the conclusion. A wonderful 'habit' of academic texts is that they nearly always refer to related influential and ground breaking papers so it is rarely difficult to track these down. The better written articles make the reader aware of counter arguments and the pitfalls of previous research. Mixed with a good dose of healthy scepticism I found it reasonably easy to get broad overviews without ever touching Medline or a text book. Recent systemic reviews and meta-analyses and the summary articles in *Drug and Therapeutic Bulletin* were especially helpful. I found *Update* and *Practitioner* did not give the depth of discussion I wanted but were useful to highlight hot topics and give references to use as the starting point when reading around a subject.

I never tried to remember references in detail. Authors names that repeatedly cropped up became important and I did commit them to memory but most of my references were vague. Examples were a paper by The Centre for Reviews and Dissemination, *Drug and Therapeutics Bulletin* last year, a chapter in the *RCGP Members Handbook*, a review article in *Effective Health Care* and the final chapter in Roger Neighbour's book. If one objective of the exam is to test our ability to read appropriately I hope my references came across as enough to highlight that I was reading effectively and 'like an interested GP' without having to clog up the old grey matter.

It is often suggested that we should be familiar with the previous 2 years of the *BMJ* and *BJGP*. During the registrar year I did get into the habit of reading these journals as they arrived (previous to this they were lucky to be taken out of the plastic wrappers) but I never read past issues. At the height of studying it would take 30 minutes to read each journal. It is strange how selective you get under pressure.

My list of hot topics was never finished. The more I read the more it grew. It is still pinned to the wall with over 50 items untouched by study. Perhaps there were subjects I should have addressed and papers that any self-respecting GP would consider neglectful not to know. In the end my attitude was that I had learned a vast amount and the objective was not to know everything but simply enough.

Another important source of information besides texts were the other members of the Primary Health Care Team. I asked the Practice Manager about the new practice leaflet, employment of staff and how to claim for items of service. The District Nurses taught me all about dressings and their costs and the Practice Nurse was grilled about her training skills. These discussions broadened my horizons, never for one second felt like revision and on a couple of occasions saved me from embarrassing silences during the viva.

Towards the end of my revision I looked at exam technique, something which is explored in detail in this book. Starting with the MEQ paper, success depends on the ability to pick out 'constructs' (major issues in the presented problem). These constructs are broad and varied but come up time and time again in different questions. For example common ones which are not immediately obvious are issues such as GPs feelings, mixed responsibilities (i.e. to the patient, the practice and society), placing the problem within context of the patient's life style and alteration of health seeking behaviour. I did enough practice MEQ papers to be able to list the common constructs and useful phrases (about 50). Then I organised these into a mind map (a cobweb of points) to help me remember them and literally trained myself to draw this out within 2 minutes from memory. At the beginning of the exam I was able to write out the mind map and use it as a reference for every one of the questions. It probably saved me 30 minutes thinking time during the 3 hour exam.

The skills of critical analysis were picked up during my revision reading. I cannot stress too much the need to be sceptical about all research. My attitudes list helped enormously by encouraging me to focus on how research and findings related to the real world of general practice. I was fortunate also that the *BMJ* was running a series of articles about critical analysis, and I did read the very short book on this subject by I.K. Crombie.

Two weeks prior to the exam I began practising MCQs. I have always felt I have underperformed in MCQs and was determined to find out why. In addition I wanted to identify those areas I was weak in, leaving myself time to address these gaps in knowledge. Critical marking helped me to realise I lost 2–3% of marks from not reading the questions correctly! After 1500 questions you can spot the subjects you drop marks in. My weak areas were drug interactions (which repeatedly came up), basic medical statistics, infective paediatric illnesses and treatment of eye complaints. This led me to some exceptionally helpful but very dull sources of information; the opening chapters and appendices in the *BNF* and some lecture notes on statistics a friend of mine had been given for the MRCP exam.

Most of the preparation for the viva was the same as for the written papers. However, in addition I concentrated on the language of ethics and looked up some recent cases which had been highlighted in the medical press. I practiced viva questions on myself, bored my family with my monologues and arranged for my own trainer and another Registrar to grill me. What I learned was that the initial subjects raised in the viva may be very varied but because examiners are encouraged to test candidates in certain areas, questions often need answering in a limited number of ways. An example of this is when the examiner presents a scenario that needs the partners, or the whole practice, to alter how they deliver a service (i.e. because of staff changes, money problems or contract changes). If you are able to recognise these scenarios as issues around the management of change the answers become very similar.

The final piece of preparation that I regret not taking seriously was being rested. There were 6 hours of written papers on the first day of the exam and I am convinced my performance related as much to the ability to continue thinking straight in a state of tiredness as it did to factual recall. It sounds a little soft but several good nights' sleep before the exam are important. My son at the time had the snuffles and wondered what had happened to his 3.00 am cuddles. Ironically after the exam he had learnt to sleep through.

My marks in the exam: MEQ–A CRQ–A MCQ–B Oral–B Video–Pass

APPENDIX 1: THE CONSULTATION

Various models have been described to help explain what happens in a consultation. The following summary of the various approaches is given to allow an overall view of the subject.

Description of events occurring in a consultation (after Byrne and Long 1976)

This model was produced after analysing over 2,000 tape recordings of consultations. They identified six phases that form a logical structure to the consultation.

- The doctor establishes a relationship with the patient
- The doctor either attempts to discover, or actually discovers, the reason for the patient's attendance
- The doctor conducts a verbal or physical examination, or both
- The doctor, or the doctor and the patient together, or the patient alone (usually in that order of probability) considers the condition
- The doctor, and occasionally the patient, details treatment or further investigation
- The consultation is terminated – usually by the doctor.

Expansion to include preventative care

In 1979 Stott and Davis described four areas which could be systematically explored each time a patient consults.

- Management of presenting problems
- Management of continuing problems
- Modification of help-seeking behaviour
- Opportunistic health promotion.

Appendix 1: The Consultation

A model of seven tasks

This model was detailed by Pendleton *et al.* in 1984. It lists seven tasks which form an effective consultation. The model emphasises the importance of the patient's view and understanding of the problem.

- To define the reasons for the patient's attendance including:
  nature and history of the problem
  cause of the problem
  patient's ideas, concerns and expectations
  effects of the problems
- To consider other problems:
  continuing problems
  risk factors
- To choose with the patient an appropriate action for each problem
- To achieve a shared understanding with the patient
- To involve the patient in the management plan and encourage him to accept appropriate responsibility
- To use time and resources appropriately
- To establish or maintain a relationship with the patient which helps to achieve the other tasks.

Health belief model

This model was devised by Rosenstock in 1966, and Becker and Maiman in 1975. It looks at the patient's reasons for accepting or rejecting the doctor's opinion. It shows that the patient is more likely to accept advice, diagnosis or treatment if the doctor is aware of his ideas, concerns and expectations.

It looks at various factors.

- Patients' interest in health varies - 'health motivation'
- Patients vary in how likely they think they are to contract an illness – 'perceived vulnerability'
- Patients' belief in the diagnosis is affected by whether they feel their opinion or 'concerns' have been understood by the doctor
- 'Perceived seriousness' varies between patients for a given condition.

Six categories of intervention

This was devised by a psychologist, John Heron, in the mid 1970s, as a model of interventions which can be used by the doctor.

- Prescriptive: instructions or advice — directive
- Informative: explaining and giving information
- Confronting: giving feedback to the patients on their behaviour or attitude, in order to help them see what is happening
- Cathartic: helping the patient to release his emotions
- Catalytic: encouraging the patient to explore his own feelings and reasons for his behaviour
- Supportive: encouraging the patient's self worth (e.g. by giving approval).

Transactional analysis

This model of communication was described by Eric Berne in the 1960s. It explores our behaviour within relationships. It identifies three 'ego-states', Parent, Adult and Child, any one of which an individual could be experiencing at any time. It looks at the implications and reasons for the different states. It also explores 'games', which can be used to identify why transactions repeatedly go wrong. This model is useful for exploring consultations by looking at the relationship between the doctor and the patient.

Balint

This work in the 1950s explored the importance of the doctor–patient relationship. It explored the importance and identification of psychological problems. It suggested the following concepts:

- The doctor as the drug
  The 'pharmacology' of the doctor as a treatment
- The child as the presenting complaint
  The patient may offer another person as the problem when there are underlying psycho-social problems
- Elimination by appropriate physical examination
  This may reinforce the patient's belief that his symptoms (neurotic in origin) are in fact due to physical illness. Repeated investigations perpetuate this cycle

- Collusion of anonymity
  As above, referral reinforces mistaken belief in the origin of symptoms. The responsibility of uncovering underlying psycho-social problems becomes increasingly diluted by repeated referral, with nobody taking final responsibility
- The Mutual Investment Company
  This is formed and managed by the doctor and the patient. 'Clinical illnesses' are episodes in a long relationship and represent 'offers' of problems (physical and psycho-social) to the doctor
- The flash
  The point in the consultation when the real reason for the 'offer' (underlying psycho-social and neurotic illness) is suddenly apparent to both doctor and patient. This forms a fulcrum for change; the consultation can now deal with the underlying basic 'fault'.

The inner consultation

This work by Roger Neighbour published in 1987 looks at improving consultation skills. He uses the following format for the consultation:

- Connecting: rapport building skills
- Summarising: listening and eliciting skills
- Handover: communicating skills
- Safety netting: predicting skills. Contingency plans of what and when further action may be needed.
- Housekeeping: taking care of yourself, checking you are ready for the next patient.

It is not suggested that you should memorise the above models, but you should have an understanding of at least some of them. You should also be aware of how you can analyse your own consultation methods and how you could work on improving them (i.e. use of video or audio tape recordings, simulated consultations with actors, role play or colleagues 'sitting in').

APPENDIX 2: MEDICAL AUDIT

This has been defined as *'the systematic critical analysis of the quality of medical care, including the procedures used for diagnosis and treatment, the use of resources and the resulting outcome and quality of care of life for the patient.'* Department of Health, January 1989. A knowledge of the basic principles is essential, not just for the exam but also for day to day practice.

Medical audit can be seen as a series of steps (The audit cycle):
- Step 1 Choose a topic and set a standard
- Step 2 Compare present practice with this standard
- Step 3 Modify your practice to make the standard attainable
- Step 4 Repeat the process to confirm improvement

Step 1

The choice of topic is vast. Involvement by all staff concerned is important, since their future commitment is paramount. Often a topic with financial implications, e.g. immunisation targets, or one in which clinical care has been questioned, e.g. sudden death can be chosen. It should be relevant to the practice's needs and lead to improved patient care. The topic can be chosen from several areas, as follows.

- Practice structure (e.g. surgery premises, range and type of equipment, the records system and organisational systems design)
- Processes (e.g. examinations undertaken, prescriptions written, tests carried out, advice given)
- Outcomes (e.g. social functioning, psychological functioning, physical functioning and patient satisfaction).

When conducting an audit a very specific question should be asked (i.e. How good is our management of hypertension?). An agreed standard is then determined, for example 80% of patients with established hypertension aged 20–35 will have a diastolic pressure less than 90 millimetres of mercury within the first year of treatment.

Step 2

Data should be collected so that it can be compared to the agreed standard.

Step 3

Collecting data is only of value if a change in practice results. The practice needs to be modified so that the agreed standard is reached. This involves team work and delegation.

Step 4

This is widely seen as the most important stage — often called 'closing the loop' since it demonstrates if improvement is actually being achieved.

An excellent introduction is given in *Making Sense of Audit* edited by Donald and Sally Irvine published by Radcliffe Medical Press Ltd.

APPENDIX 3: EVIDENCE BASED MEDICINE

Increasingly, all doctors are being asked to base their decision making on the best available scientific evidence. Unfortunately we often find that our textbooks are out of date and there is a vast amount of journal articles which may hold our answers. The articles in the journals will either be review articles or original studies and trials. These trials and studies are of variable quality and it is often difficult to know whether their results can be relied on. Evidence based medicine has been defined as 'the process of systematically finding, appraising, and using contemporaneous research findings as a basis for clinical decisions'.

The practice of evidence based medicine involves four steps:

- Step 1   Accurate identification of the clinical question to be investigated
- Step 2   A search of the literature to select relevant articles
- Step 3   Evaluation of the evidence presented in the literature
- Step 4   Implementation of the findings in clinical practice

Each of the stages requires certain skills, and these may be assessed in the Critical Reading component and Current Awareness component of papers 1 and 2, but also to some extent in the oral examination. For example, the clinical problem may be to decide at what level of blood pressure a 28-year-old female patient should be advised not to commence the oral contraceptive pill. This is a reasonable question but may not be answerable by reference to the literature. There may be studies that look at the risk factors for hypertension in young women on the oral contraceptive pill but no level of BP may be stated. We thus would need to modify our question so that we can actually search for the appropriate evidence.

The next stage of searching for evidence requires skills in searching literature databases (e.g. Medline). This usually requires a particular search strategy commonly using key words. If the appropriate key words are not selected then insufficient evidence may be presented.

Once the appropriate articles are obtained they must then be appraised, another skill which is assessed in the MRCGP examination. Finally a judgement has to be made, based on the quality of evidence and how this answers the clinical problem.

There are a number of study designs, and they are not equal with respect to the strength of their evidence. These studies can be ranked to produce a crude hierarchy of evidence, giving more weight to studies that are less vulnerable to bias.

Hierarchy of evidence

1 Well designed randomised control trial (the gold standard)
2 Other types of trials   a) well designed control trials without randomisation
                  b) cohort (prospective study)
                  c) case-control (retrospective study)
3 Epidemiological observational studies
4 Opinions of respected authorities based on clinical experience, including reports of expert committees

No doctor in the future will be able to get far without understanding the principles of evidence based medicine. It is now an established part of the clear remit of health care managers. To simplify matters, doctors and health care managers can now refer to authoritative reviews which have used an evidence based approach.

APPENDIX 4: ETHICAL PROBLEM SOLVING

Every day we make numerous ethical decisions. Some are based on well known legal or professional codes (e.g. prescribing contraception for the under 16s), but most lack such clarity (e.g. how much information do I tell the patient about the side-effects of a course of antibiotics?). The possession of a clear understanding of the principles of ethics, and how they affect management, is vital for everyday practice and is something which is essential for the MRCGP candidate.

Ethics is the science of morals and involves:
1   the application of ethical principles on which moral values and rules are based.
2   the use of decision making skills in applying moral principles to practical problems.

All doctors need skills to enable them to recognise dilemmas, analyse them, arrive at sound conclusions and take appropriate action. We may respond intuitively but this may be inconsistent and not the result of a thorough analysis, especially with more complex issues. If we aspire to provide the best care to our patients we need to consider the underlying fundamental ethical principles and use them whenever we have to solve problems.

Ethical decision making, where we critically reflect upon the process of making our decisions, is especially important in certain areas.
*   On entering unfamiliar territory. New situations challenge our usual way of looking at problems and hence our decision making
*   When faced with greater than usual personal responsibility. Such situations challenge our decision making
*   When choosing a particular option may exclude other options, thereby having far-reaching consequences
*   When there exists a genuine moral dilemma, with painful choices having to be made between two unacceptable moral outcomes.

Fundamental ethical principles

The German philosopher Immanuel Kant argued that the concept of 'person' is fundamental to ethics. Without the concept of a person, an individual who is the bearer of rights and responsibilities, ethics cannot get started. Such individuals must always be treated as ends in themselves and this concept of a person underpins our fundamental ethical principles.

The principle of respect for persons
- The duty to respect the rights, autonomy and dignity of the person
- The duty to promote their well being and autonomy
- The duty of truthfulness, honesty and sincerity.

The principle of justice
- The duty of universal fairness or equity
- The duty to treat people as ends, never simply as means to an end
- The duty to avoid discrimination, abuse or exploitation of people on grounds of race, age, class, gender or religion.

The principle of beneficence (or non-maleficence)
- The duty to do good and avoid doing harm to others
- The duty to the vulnerable.

The concept of beneficence can be widened to encompass the duty to inform and educate, enhancing the patient's ability to continue to care for him or herself.

Ethics in context

Ethical problems do not exist in isolation, and whenever an ethical decision is under consideration it is important to be aware of the legal framework that society works under, and the professional codes that affect both the doctor and any other health care professionals who are working for the benefit of the patient.

The advice of the General Medical Council

The basic rules under which a doctor is licensed to practise by the GMC can be obtained from the various publications that it gives free to all doctors. There are certain standards of professional conduct and these fall into the following areas.

- Abuse of professional privileges
- Conduct derogatory to the reputation of the profession
- Personal relationships between doctors and patients
- Professional confidence, including disclosure of medical information and confidentiality
- Advertising of doctors' services
- Financial relationships between doctors and independent organisations providing clinical, diagnostic or medical advisory services
- Relationships between the medical profession and the pharmaceutical and allied industries.

ETHICAL PROBLEM SOLVING SEQUENCE

a) Identify the interrelations between the four factors in the social context in which the doctor is practising.

1 Situation — Different considerations have to be made if the patient is unconscious or mentally incapable of decision. There is also the wider role of community responsibility.
2 Role — The doctor's role in each of the above situations will be different.
3 Rules — There may be specific rules applying to each individual case and these are based on the law and on regulations laid down by the GMC.
4 Arbiters — There is a need to consider who the doctor is responsible or accountable to for the decision making – in other words the arbiter of our actions. This may include the patient, the GMC and the courts.

b) Apply the above to the specific ethical situation. The four components of the problem solving process are as follows.

1. Assessment — What are the crucial facts of the case? What moral principles are at issue?

2. Planning — Identify the options and goals aimed for. What is the primary aim or good for which we are aiming? What benefits and moral goals are achievable? What previous cases should we take into account? What are the right means to reach our goal?

3. Implementation — Decision and commitment to action. Consider the cost/benefit of the intervention.

4. Evaluation — Assess the outcomes, costs and benefits. How do we review the pros and cons for the action taken? Can a reasonable ethical justification be made for the course of action taken?

Example of ethical problem solving

Tom is a 22-year-old patient with schizophrenia who lives with his elderly parents. He regularly defaults from his long-acting anti psychotic injections and in the last few weeks has developed some delusions.

You receive a telephone call from a police station where he has been taken, having been found wandering in the streets. You are asked to discuss Tom's medical background by a man who states he is Tom's solicitor. Tom is apparently due to appear before the magistrate the next morning.

Ethical dilemma — Should I give medical information to the man requesting information?

Points to consider — The primary duty is to the patient.

1. Respect for patient. Need to be aware of the aspect of confidentiality and also the patient's autonomy, despite being possibly mentally ill.

2. Beneficence/Maleficence — consider the principle of doing good versus doing harm.

3. Consider the GMC rules on confidentiality, the Mental Health Act and the responsibility under this.

Intervention

1. Establish mental state of Tom — need to visit police surgeon or last person to see him and information from relatives. Ask to speak to Tom.

2   Establish that the caller is in fact Tom's solicitor — ask to ring back. Check credentials and clarify who the solicitor is representing.

3   Consider own ethics — working in the best interests of the patient.

There is no right or wrong answer but the good doctor will highlight what legal and ethical principles are at stake, identify various interventions, consider the possible consequences of these interventions and finally make a 'best approach'.

Further reading
Seedhouse D *Ethics —The Heart of Health Care.* John Wiley, Chichester 1988.
Duties of a Doctor, General Medical Council, 1996.
Medical Ethics Today; its practice and philosophy, BMA, London 1997.

APPENDIX 5: RECOMMENDED READING LIST

Audit
Making Sense of Audit edited by D. and S. Irvine, 2nd edition, Radcliffe Medical Press, 1997.

The consultation
The Doctors Communication Handbook 2 edited by P. Tate, 2nd edition, Radcliffe Medical Press, 1997.
The Inner Consultation R. Neighbour, Petroc Press, 1997.

Critical appraisal
The Pocket Guide to Critical Appraisal I.K. Crombie, BMJ Publishing Group, 1996.

Basic Epidemiology R.Beaglehole, R.Bonita and T. Kjellstrom, World Health Organisation, 1993, available through HMSO.

Essential Statistics for Medical Examinations C. Marguerie and B. Faragher, PasTest 1998.

Practice management
Numerous titles.
Excellent series in Business Side of General Practice all published by Radcliffe Medical Press.

Ethics
Ethics, The Heart of Health Care D. Seedhouse, 2nd edition, John Wiley, 1998.

Doctors, Dilemmas, Decisions B. Essex, BMJ publishing, 1994.

Clinical topics
Excellent series in Oxford General Practice series published by Oxford University Press.
Excellent series ABC, BMJ Publishing Group.

Therapeutics
The British National Formulary, BMA and Pharmaceutical Society.

DHSS Publications
Drug Tariff, 1997.
Immunisation against Infectious Disease, 1996.
Handbook of Contraceptive Services.
Medical Evidence for Social Security Purposes, issued by House of Commons, 1997.

APPENDIX 6: REVISION CHECKLIST

It is helpful to produce your own revision checklist. The list will vary for each person, but should be open to addition as topical areas arise. You may like to produce a list for a group of people taking the exam and share out the topics to produce a set of summaries. In devising your list, review the Five Areas of General Practice, page xiv to make sure you cover them all. You will find some areas are well known to you and can be left off your list while others require more work. For topics such as 'Cholesterol' there is currently research being carried out and it is useful to have a list of up-to-date views on the subject. The following checklist covers most of the important areas.

- [ ] AIDS
- [ ] Alcohol and drug abuse
- [ ] Audit
- [ ] Cholesterol
- [ ] Computerisation
- [ ] Consultation (structure, length etc)
- [ ] Coping with your own anger and stress
- [ ] Counselling
- [ ] Depression
- [ ] Doctor — Patient relationship
- [ ] Effects of social class on illness
- [ ] GP obstetrics
- [ ] Hypertension
- [ ] Management of common conditions (e.g. sore throat, ear infections, UTI)
- [ ] Osteoporosis
- [ ] Paediatric surveillance
- [ ] Patient participation
- [ ] Patients' rights and complaints procedures
- [ ] Reaccreditation tests for GPs
- [ ] Resuscitation
- [ ] Risks and benefits of the oral contraceptive pill and HRT
- [ ] Role of the Practice Nurse
- [ ] Screening (children, adults, elderly, breast, cervical etc)
- [ ] Sexual abuse
- [ ] Sick doctors
- [ ] Structure of the NHS
- [ ] Terminal care

APPENDIX 7: MULTIPLE CHOICE QUESTION INDEX

Numbers shown refer to answer numbers.

PASTEST COURSES

MRCGP Weekend Courses (London and Manchester)

These courses are run by Royal College Examiners and are designed to cover all aspects of the new modular exam: MCQ Paper, Problem Solving, Critical Reading, Consulting Skills and Orals. Stimulating discussion helps candidates to refine their last-minute revision plans. Practice questions are forwarded for completion before the course.

DRCOG Three Day Courses (London and Manchester)

These courses cover all parts of the syllabus in Obstetrics, Gynaecology, Family Planning and Paediatrics. Two complete circuits of OSCEs offer invaluable experience to candidates and a revision checklist is provided. Practice questions are forwarded for completion before the course.

DCH Five Day Courses (London)

This intensive course covers all aspects of paediatrics required for this Diploma, including the clinical examination. The extensive lecture notes and handouts are based on past exam questions. Pre-course material is provided.

PasTest has been established in the field of postgraduate medical education since 1972 providing revision books and intensive study courses for doctors preparing for their professional examinations. Books and courses are available for the following specialties:
MRCP Part 1 and Part 2 (General Medicine and Paediatrics), MRCOG, DRCOG, MRCGP, DCH, FRCA, FRCS and PLAB.

For further details contact:
PasTest, Freepost, Knutsford, Cheshire WA16 7BR
Tel: 01565 755226   Fax: 01565 650264

PASTEST COURSES

PASTEST the key to exam success, the key to your future

PasTest is dedicated to helping doctors to pass their professional examinations. We have 25 years of specialist experience in medical education and over 3000 doctors attend our revision courses each year.

Experienced lecturers:
Many of our lecturers are also examiners and teach in a lively and interesting way in order to:

- reflect current trends in exams
- give plenty of mock exam practice
- provide essential advice on exam technique

Outstanding accelerated learning:
Our up-to-date and relevant course material includes MCQs, colour slides, X-rays, ECGs, EEGs, clinical cases, data interpretations, mock exams, vivas and extensive course notes which provide:

- hundreds of high quality MCQs with detailed answers and explanations
- succinct notes, diagrams and charts

Personal attention:
Active participation is encouraged on these courses, so in order to give personal tuition and to answer individual questions our course numbers are limited.
Book early to avoid disappointment.

Choice of courses:
PasTest has developed a wide range of high quality interactive courses in different cities around the UK to suit your individual needs.

What other students have said about our courses:
'Absolutely brilliant - I would not have passed without it! Thank you.'
Dr Charitha Rajapakse, London.
'Excellent, enjoyable, extremely hard work but worth every penny.'
Dr Helen Binns, Oxford.

PasTest, Egerton Court, Parkgate Estate,
Knutsford, Cheshire WA16 8DX, UK.
Telephone: 01565 755226   Fax: 01565 650264
e-mail: pastest@dial.pipex.com
web site: http:\\www.pastest.co.uk

EAST GLAMORGAN GENERAL HOSPITAL

CHURCH VILLAGE, near

236